THE
PASTORS'
BARRACKS

THE PASTORS'

△

BARRACKS

ROBERT L. WISE

VICTOR BOOKS

A DIVISION OF SCRIPTURE PRESS PUBLICATIONS INC.
USA CANADA ENGLAND

Library of Congress Catalog Card Number: 85-62712
ISBN: 0-89693-157-9

© 1986 by SP Publications, Inc. All rights reserved
Printed in the United States of America

VICTOR BOOKS A division of SP Publications, Inc. Wheaton, Illinois 60187

CONTENTS △

Dedicated to

Lulu Jane Moses
who taught me that all good
things come to those who trust God
. . . and wait patiently

FOREWORD △

THE RECORD OF THE CHURCH in Germany during the Nazi era is still being pieced together. It is a story of embarrassment and failure, but also of determination and steadfastness. The church was unprepared for the powerful propaganda which the Nazis unleashed, and was slow in answering the ideological challenge.

There was the futile attempt of the German-Christian church that sought to accommodate Nazi ideology and defend it theologically. There were the pietistic churches, characterized by their nonpolitical bent, which by and large continued a quiet yet active church life. And there were Protestant theologians and pastors who articulated a biblical critique of the regime—these became known as the Confessing Church and suffered as adversaries. In reality, the lines between the three positions were not always clearly marked. Human fear and political bewilderment caused many Christians to tolerate Nazi ideology, even admire some of Hitler's successes, while at the same time displaying evangelical fervor.

Against the backdrop of such confusion, the names of

Bonhoeffer, Dibeilius, and Niemöller often have been cited as prophetic voices of faith and uncompromising obedience to God. What about other Christians?

Robert Wise's account of the Pomeranian village pastor and Dachau inmate, Christian Reger, offers an insider's view of the church during the Nazi regime. Reger's credibility—as a respresentative of Christians in Nazi Germany who lived by their convictions—becomes firmly established in our minds. Yet this unpretentious man was only one of many pastors and priests in Dachau's barracks. Through them we learn the real meaning of courage as well as of the struggle within the German church.

The strength of this book on the Holocaust lies in the fact that it encompasses a period extending beyond Hitler's reign and provides an uncommon perspective, that of Christians learning to live and think with each other while victims of powerful political forces, first Nazism, then Communism.

A skillful storyteller, Robert Wise has deep human insights and expands our understanding of true Christianity. I have benefited greatly from reading this book and feel a particular bond to it, because I grew up in Nazi Germany, only a few kilometers from Stieglitz, the same village in which Christian Reger pastored.

FRIEDHELM RADANDT, President
The King's College
Briarcliff Manor,
New York

PREFACE △

I FIRST MET CHRISTIAN REGER in 1978 at Dachau Concentration Camp. Each day he shared the history of the camp with the many people who came to visit the memorial chapel located behind the idle crematoriums. As chaplain, he was always available to answer questions about what imprisonment had meant—and he knew firsthand.

By 1978, the camp had become a respectable, sterilized memorial as well as a remembrance of its own macabre statistics. It was a reminder that the Nazis had either directly or indirectly caused the deaths of at least 25 million Russians, 12 million Germans, and 6 million Jews, not counting the deaths of the rest of the Allied Forces. Dachau Concentration Camp and Christian Reger were also reminders that the vast majority of the citizens of the Third Reich had quietly acquiesced to Adolf Hitler's reign of terror. Of the few protesters and resisters to National Socialism, many were sent to Dachau.

No one knows how many died at Dachau as political prisoners, for the Nazis purposefully obscured the records. But at least 10 percent of the inmates were clergy. This unique flock of men were housed together in the "Pastors' Barracks," and this book is based on their experiences.

These good men were caught in the crossfire of treacherous times and lived in the midst of deceit, fear, and violence. These were common people who had to choose. Because they chose to be brave when they were afraid, to be true when surrounded by lies, and to look when others hid their eyes, they became uncommon.

In particular, this is the story of one man who only wanted to live a quiet, simple existence. His dreams and intentions were for the routine life of the quaint, pastoral German village. Yet as the storm clouds gathered over Europe in the closing days of 1939, he followed his convictions and descended into the fiercest maelstrom of the 20th century.

Standing before the foundations of the Pastors' Barracks, I wondered why they had said no to National Socialism while the rest looked the other way. From whence came their courage when others manifested only cowardice? What secrets of strength might their spirits still share with me? My quest for answers to these questions led me to my friendship with Christian Reger.

As we corresponded over a number of years, the bits and pieces of his story fell together. I began to experience how a serious and sensitive boy grew into manhood, went to seminary, and found his way to a small parish in Stieglitz. I was warmed by the marvelous love story of his courtship with Mina and their separation during his years in prison. A new perspective on the meaning of suffering began to take shape in my mind. Christian Reger helped me discover what true valor means.

Moreover, I found in this story the recurrent theme of the confrontation between good and evil that ebbs and flows through every generation. The deeds of the Nazis mirrored in an extraordinary way the predictions of the Book of Revelation that many times throughout history the eternal clash would break through the boundaries of time and take on an ultimate dimension of Tribulation. In such an hour, the Beast himself would descend on the saints, bent on obliterating them from the face of the earth. When the Third Reich and National Socialism arose from the Pit, they came with such intentions. Into this apocalyptic moment came Christian Reger and his friends. Their endurance instructs!

I want you to know this story because its meaning may be of crucial importance in a yet distant day of decision. Perhaps truth will again be on the scaffold and you will be called to choose to stand for the right. In that critical hour, this story of another person who maintained the courage and convictions of faith may come to mind.

The last time I saw Christian Reger was in Amsterdam. We read through the manuscript and talked about the people in this story and what had become of them. He assured me that none of the faithful had shrunk back. As I studied his unpretentious manner and listened to his honest, direct speech, I was reminded of how deceptive ordinariness can be. I tried to etch his face into my mind so that in a moment of crisis I might recall that worn but steady countenance again. Christian Reger will always remain for me a portrait in courage.

My deepest special appreciation is extended to the three people who helped with the development of this manuscript. Many years ago Dorothy Waltz helped compile much of the initial material. Jan Wolfard typed the final manuscript and Jeannie Rogers helped with the final editing. I thank them all very much.

ROBERT L. WISE
Oklahoma City,
Oklahoma
1985

CHAPTER ONE △

THE BEAST YET ALIVE—1946

EVEN THE COLORS of the matchbox were the same as the one that had been slipped into his hand in prison. The red and green cover had a hypnotic effect on Christian Reger as he watched the box in the bishop's hand. He felt as if he were seeing a mystical reappearance of an old token of hope.

"We believe this is an hour of unprecedented importance," Bishop Dibeilius stressed, tapping the box forcefully against the large oak desk. The movement of red and green caused Christian's attention to drift away. After all, his very life had been sustained by the matchbox.

"Few people have seen, much less lived through, what has been your daily experience for the last five years." The bishop's voice betrayed a slight irritation because he sensed he was not receiving the full attention he normally enjoyed. "Great strength and courage were required to have resisted and endured as you have."

Christian got out of his chair and limped to the window. *Perhaps if I look in some other direction,* he thought, *I will not be as distracted.* From the window he saw skeletons of steel and stone that stood as ravaged monuments to the past glory of Berlin.

"Reger, you have been the recipient of enormous gifts of grace," the bishop added, rising from behind his desk.

"Well," Christian finally answered, "grace sometimes comes to us best in small things."

The matchbox came to his mind again. When he had first been arrested, the terror had been almost unbearable. Later, as imprisonment had eaten away his self-confidence, an unshakable depression had settled into his soul. It was in the darkest moment of despair that the matchbox had been slipped into his hand. When he had opened it and found the piece of paper with the special message, his sanity had been restored. Such a small object—and yet it had meant so much!

"Christian," Bishop Dibeilius continued, bearing down hard now, "there is no question that you are the man for this position." The bishop paused as he studied the face of the pastor who seemed so unmoved by his status. Reger's sunken brown eyes were underlined by dark circles. Much of his dark brown hair had grown back, but its straight-back style seemed to belong to a man who didn't worry about making an impression. There was no sign of retreat or hesitance in his face, but clearly a deep tiredness was etched on his mouth and high forehead. Reger still possessed the muscular look of an athlete, but now his clothes hung limply on his thin frame.

"We truly believe you can go into the new Russian sector of Berlin and be most effective."

"Thank you, Bishop." Christian smiled politely. "I am honored by your confidence in me." Now he studied the man before him with his well-combed gray hair and carefully trimmed mustache. Though the bishop's coat was now several years old, it still had a flair that set him apart as one of the upper class. Even in this room stripped of every luxury, the bishop remained a striking reflection of the days of the kaisers.

14

"However," Reger continued, "I am not sure that any German is going to be acceptable to the Communists. We are living in a new world and the old order is gone forever."

"Oh, but that is exactly my point! Because you were imprisoned and the German courts declared you to be an enemy of the Nazis, you are a man for this new day."

Once more the bishop took measure of his man. There was nothing pretentious or ostentatious about Christian Reger. Yet his penetrating glances left no doubt about his intelligence. Simple rimless glasses added to an impression of studiousness; the strong set of his jaw with its cleft chin conveyed determination; and his prominent nose completed the appearance of one who has an inner ability to set his will and not be moved.

"The Communists would let a man like yourself work when other men would be harassed or arrested," the bishop concluded.

Slowly Reger sat down again as if he were bargaining for time to avoid the inevitable. "Bishop, I have been through so much during these last years, that I am not sure I have the strength left in me. Perhaps I will never be completely free of my physical problems."

The bishop sighed heavily, no longer able to find the right words for his arguments. He remembered how he had refused to believe the stories about the concentration camps. He recalled conversations in which bishops assured each other of the great promise National Socialism held for the church. He thought of how long he had waited before taking any public stand. Yet he could let his mind drift only so far. Then like a steel curtain abruptly falling, those thoughts were sealed away. Yet as much as he tried to dismiss any vestiges of those memories, a vague embarrassment remained.

"I'm sure I cannot appreciate what your condition has been or what your wife Mina has lived through." He slowly sat down behind the desk again. "I asked her to wait outside because I

15

didn't want to say anything that might disturb her. Of course, I have received reports of her exemplary leadership in the parish. I am truly sorry for what she has. . . ." For the first time the bishop's voice lost its self-assurance and started to fade. "I understand that Mina . . . that she has suffered greatly.

"Your examples are what we need right now!" The bishop had found his official voice once more. "You are an ideal that people can follow."

"I am no example!" Christian snapped, and then stopped as his eyes became moist. "I have merely survived. I have done only what had to be done. Many others did much more and they are gone. We have survived and that is all."

"No, Christian," the bishop said softly but firmly. "I cannot agree. Few people have stood where you have walked. I know of your deeds in the camp and they speak for themselves. Your life's work is the essence of what we profess."

Christian shifted his weight in the chair and looked at the floor. As long as the conversation seemed austere, he could easily resist the pressure, but when the praise was honest and personal, he felt awkward and unsure of what to say.

"I know I have no right to ask you to go," the bishop went on, "yet I have no one else of your stature to send. Truly, you have wrestled with the Dragon and have survived. Such a credential is earned only through fire, pain, and anguish. I cannot ignore the possibilities your background offers. Now that the Beast has arisen again among us, we must send only our best warriors to the battle."

As Christian rubbed his hands together and felt how leathery they still were, his eyes once more fell on the matchbox now resting squarely in the middle of the desk.

"I am a simple parish pastor," he feebly protested. "I came to Stieglitz in 1931 after I had been out of seminary only a year and served there until I was arrested in 1940. I have not been in many places."

"Berliners who will have to live under the heavy hand of the Beast will not need a great theologian to answer profound questions. In their world they will not require some fine orator to impress the congregation with flowery speech. They must have a man who knows the truth and who will not compromise in his obedience.

"Before the war I studied the lives of the saints and martyrs. I suppose it was sort of a hobby," the bishop reminisced. "I was intrigued by the people who said yes under terrible circumstances. I wondered what made them stand firm when all the others were running. Of course, their courage was what made these ordinary people extraordinary. However, I found I could never quite grasp their secrets." His voice trailed off in reflection and then came back with painful honesty. "I was too sophisticated, too complicated, too calculating. I knew I could always find good reasons to say no."

"It was very hard for any of us to decide the right thing to do," Christian replied, trying to minimize the bishop's self-deprecation. "None of us could know how very complex matters were. We were all deceived in many ways."

"It took great strength to say yes." The bishop ignored the consolation and excuses being offered him.

"Sometimes the yes comes about by simply saying no to evil. Such answers are not really so difficult."

"Was it really that simple?" The bishop motioned with his hand to keep Christian from speaking. He was clearly not going to take no for an answer. He needed someone to go to East Berlin and he knew he was looking at the right man.

"Oh, yes, we have all lived through hard days during these last years of the war," the bishop continued. "Many have had little or no food. Certainly every family has lost someone or perhaps everything. But those of you who survived the concentration camps have survived hell itself. You were not there because you deserved punishment, but because you stood for the truth And that is a profound difference."

"I will not minimize what happened to those of us who were there," Christian said. "The memory of our fallen comrades would be poorly served if I did."

"I can honestly tell you that most of us had no idea that the conditions in the camps were so horrible."

"Oh?" Hidden within the inflections of Christian's voice was a sound that interrogated. His eyes narrowed and his gaze became intense.

"Well, I mean—" the bishop fumbled for words, "I mean, we, or at least *I*, didn't know. People, ah, er, people didn't talk of such things."

"Oh?" Reger's question continued to question.

"Of course, there were rumors, but confirmation was not possible." The bishop suddenly gestured forcefully as a preacher might when trying to camouflage a weak point. "And what could I have done anyway?"

"Of course." Reger seemed to confirm his excuses.

"Surviving was the point, wasn't it?" the bishop pleaded. "We all had to do what was necessary to live, didn't we? What good would have been accomplished if we had all been swept away? Compromise is an essential and unavoidable part of life. After all, courage is very difficult to define."

"I make no claims on courage," Christian returned. "I'm not sure that I even understand what it is."

"Oh, but you do!" the bishop insisted. "You do! You must. You survived because of your courage."

"Survival is always a gift of grace." Christian's smile exposed spaces where teeth had been. "Compromise and courage have nothing to do with whether the heart continues to beat or not. Cowards have lived when better men were being lowered into their graves. *Whether* we live or die is God's business. *How* we stay alive is our business."

"See! See? You understand the matters that Berliners must

now live with every hour of their lives. People will respect you. You have earned the right to speak of such questions. Your whole life has been a preparation for these days that are before us."

Instantly a myriad of thoughts crowded Christian's mind. During the *vez sacrum*, the holy spring of spiritual renewal in the days of his youth, the message had come of Herman Schmidt's death in the World War. The boyish face of the young man he had so greatly admired came into sharp focus as Christian momentarily felt again the experience of Herman's death. He remembered how he had begun to think of becoming a pastor so that he too could comfort people. He remembered his mother crying because their bread was gone when ravishing inflation had destroyed the value of their money. He felt the fear that had surged through their village when talk of a Communist uprising had been feverish. From yet another decade, the sounds of shouting filled his inner ears and once more he saw doors flying open and SS troops rushing into the church's secret assemblies. Then another collage of faces assembled before him as Karl Leisner, Werner Sylten, Wilhelm Dittner, Heinrich Gruber, Helmut Hesse, and a multitude of comrades from the camp marched on review across his mind. As they passed, it seemed as if their searching eyes probed his integrity.

"I said," the bishop repeated himself, "your whole life has been a preparation for this assignment."

"I suppose it has," Christian said slowly, sounding more and more convinced. "You are right, Bishop. Evil has cast a long shadow over my entire life."

"I am sorry that the Beast is not dead, Christian. The battle is not over. Regardless of what we have done right or wrong, we must all go on from here. Whether the price we paid is great or small does not change the issues at hand." Sensing that he had almost persuaded his man, the bishop nervously reached over and picked up the matchbox again. "Now will you say yes?"

THE PASTORS' BARRACKS
△

Reger's eyes moved from the red and green box to the massive wooden door that led out of the room. As he looked at the door, another image floated before his eyes—a door that had opened in 1940 to plunge him into a world of terror and chaos.

CHAPTER TWO △

DESCENT
INTO HELL—1940

One

THE ENTIRE BOXCAR ROCKED as the huge wooden door was slid to a thudding halt. Days and days of riding with only slits of light coming through the cracks had caused the men's eyes to adjust to near total darkness. Suddenly daylight flooded into the car with such brilliance that no one's eyes could tolerate it. Christian felt stabbing pain in both eyes and shielded his head only to be confronted by the stench that seemed to arise from the floor.

The hay had become foul during their first week of transportation and in the summer heat each subsequent day only made the smell worse. The odors of hot, sweaty bodies and unemptied urinal buckets mingled together to become an almost visible blanket of suffocation. When at last the door opened, Christian gulped down the breeze in relief.

Beyond the boxcar doorway, chaos prevailed. Dogs were barking, men were shouting, and hordes of prisoners were tramping off somewhere. Like some great whirlpool sucking life down into its depths, the whole process seemed to be pulling the prisoners closer and closer to the point of no return.

"Hurry up, you swine! Everybody out!" The ear-shattering screech of a police whistle punctuated the commands. "Quickly, you fools. Out!"

Immediately, the prisoners in the front of the boxcar began piling out onto the sidewalks. The surge of pushing and shoving carried Christian forward, and as the fresh air hit his face, he tried to purge his lungs. For the first time he glimpsed the concrete docks and the barbed wire-lined corridors in front of him. Dismay, disorientation, and apprehension swept through his mind.

"No waiting! Move!" The SS officers strutted back and forth, barking orders and kicking at the men as they passed. "Faster! Now! Quickly!" accompanied the constant snarling and barking of ferocious guard dogs, whose taut leashes were relaxed whenever a slashing bite might serve to quicken the pace. Men stumbled and stepped on each other as the press of the crowd pushed them onward.

A small Jew, whose acquaintance Christian had made during the long weeks of riding, suddenly lost his footing and fell from the car, sprawling onto the tracks. As Christian instinctively started to jump from the car to help the man, a hand grabbed his arm from behind and held him back.

Immediately, an SS guard jumped down from the concrete dock and smashed his large rubber club down across the Jew's back, flattening the prisoner against the ground.

"Welcome! Welcome to Dachau!" the guard screamed at all of them and hit the Jew again.

"Those who have trouble moving, I help!" And he dug the toe of his black leather boot into the man's ribs. "Those who don't try to conform, I teach to adjust!" He grabbed the back of the Jew's collar and slung him into the curbing. As the Jew's body slid along the side of the wall, the top of his head scraped the cement.

Christian strained forward again as his whole being wrenched in violent inward protest against the brutality. Though he had already been in custody several months, he still could not think of himself as a prisoner. His arms ached to stop the clubbing and kicking, but the hidden hand restrained him. He turned to see Wilhelm Dittner holding tightly to his coat sleeve.

"Try something and they will beat you to death," he growled. "I know what I'm talking about."

Christian searched the dirty, tired face of this strange man who had become his friend as the train rumbled across Germany. The stubble of his unshaven beard had long since transformed the handsome appearance of this fellow clergyman into that of exiled drifter. Dittner's cold, hard eyes clearly spelled out the truth. He had been a prisoner much longer and seen cruelty much worse than Christian could conceive. Christian's tense muscles went slack and he tried to look the other way.

The whole carload of men had stopped in place during the beating, but the pause was only momentary. The press of the emptying car swept Reger past the Jew lying on the ground.

"Faster! Faster! Faster!" echoed from all sides. The guards had a mania for speeding up the process. As best as Reger could tell, they were being pushed into a converging narrow walkway that only packed the prisoners more tightly together.

He stumbled twice and could feel a sharp sting in his knee. Yet he dare not look but only keep trotting through the entrance-way. The route turned and opened before a huge metal gate. The flow of men stopped as they spread out again in the open area before the gate.

The image of the little Jew lying face down on the ground came back. He could see the man trying to cover his head from the blows while his legs thrashed up and down from the pain. Conversations they had had in the train returned.

"You can live through this," he had assured Christian. "My people have lived through such for centuries. The secret is to have a strong enough reason to live and then you will."

"Is survival so simple?" Christian asked innocently.

"Certainly it is hard, but it is possible," the Jew had insisted. "Nietzsche has said, 'He who has a *why* to live can bear almost any *how* he must endure.' If you believe enough you can survive."

Bewilderment swept away Christian's memories. Never in his life had he experienced or even imagined the possibility of what had happened to him during the last several weeks and especially in the past few minutes. Anger and confusion seemed to blend together into an emotional muddle that left him immobilized.

Yet the crowd inched forward. Like an hourglass constrictor slowing down the sand, the gateway was delaying their march. Christian looked up and saw huge letters atop the wrought-iron gate: "*Arbeit Macht Frei.*"

"So, 'Work Makes You Free' here," a voice coarsely whispered in his ear. "I bet it will also make you dead."

He turned his head to discover Dittner directly behind him. His six-foot frame made him tower over Christian even though he certainly didn't seem that much heavier or more muscular. His thick black hair and deep-blue eyes were striking. Christian had learned that his fellow prisoner and pastor friend often spoke with irony to conceal a deep bitterness that lurked only slightly below the surface.

"They might better have written, 'Welcome to the Dragon's Lair,'" Dittner snarled.

"Shut up, you vermin!" a guard screamed from somewhere. "Stop that talking and get this line moving! Now!"

Squeezing past the iron gate, Christian found himself inside a courtyard that ended in front of the *Jourhaus,* the administrative building. Another voice muttered, "Maybe the sign should read, 'Give up hope, you who enter here.'"

"You are being processed in the Jourhaus!" a loudspeaker boomed overhead. "Move quickly; we have no time for delays!"

Once again an invisible whirlpool began to suck the men into another entryway, pulling Christian along with it. But as he stepped through the doorway, a fist suddenly smashed against the side of his face, smacking him against the door jamb.

"Swine! You are not here for a vacation!" a faceless voice yelled. "Take off your hat and stop delaying the line." Stunned, terrified, and stinging, he shuffled ahead aimlessly until the line abruptly halted.

As Christian felt the welt swelling on the side of his head, he remembered another attack enroute to the camp. In Mannheim, as the manacled prisoners were being moved to a different cattle car, a man bolted across the train platform and struck the prisoner in front of Christian. As the prisoner fell, the man who had struck him turned his fury on Christian.

"Traitors!" he screamed in Reger's face. "How dare you oppose our Führer!" With his umbrella, the businessman began swinging in every direction. The guards watched and did nothing. "You should be castrated for this!" he screeched at the man behind Christian. "Your disrespect for Adolf Hitler is vile!"

Having spent his anger, the businessman walked back into the watching crowd. The guard merely tipped his hat to the man as if nodding his appreciation for a service well rendered.

As Christian's mind snapped back to the present, he discovered he was standing in a line, his mouth hanging open, and his eyes staring blankly ahead. Pushed, shoved, harassed, he went past information tables and questioners. Jerked in front of a camera, he was hit again and pushed on to another part of the administration building and then to the dressing room. There Christian's clothes were removed and piled into the heaps strewn along the walls. Left with only his belt, he stood naked in another line.

"In here! Step up quickly," a prisoner insisted. Before Christian were a number of men in prison garb standing ready with razors, scissors, and clippers. They seized the new inmates and quickly began shaving their heads. In a matter of minutes each man had had his hair peeled from his entire body. Immediately, Christian discovered that the endless flow of men had dulled the razors and scissors so that he felt as if half his hair had been pulled out.

At the far end of the "barber shop" were showers and on the other side were the striped prison uniforms and wooden clogs each man was to wear. Stripped of his possessions, his head and body aching and bald, Christian realized that the uniform did little to keep him from still feeling naked.

His eyes searched about the dressing room for a familiar face. He was surrounded by other bald, white-skulled, and degraded men. Not one person was recognizable to him. *Perhaps,* he thought, *I have had many conversations with some of these men during the trip here yet I don't know them. Every sign of individuality is gone.* He groaned as he realized that he too had taken on a strangely anonymous appearance. He felt as if he were being swallowed up by his surroundings.

"They are trying to make us into animals," he confided to a blank face before him. "We are being stripped of all dignity," he complained, but the face only stared back.

Once again the mass of men turned into a line and Christian was moved on before another interrogator. "Name!" the guard barked. "Your name!"

"Reger," he answered haltingly. "Christian Reger."

"No longer!" the guard snapped back without even looking up from his clipboard. "You are now number 26 661. You are not worthy of a name. Only when you are proven ready to reenter German society will your name be given back."

"But . . . " Christian tried to protest.

"Move on, 26 661!"

"Your crime?" the next guard demanded.

"Political, I suppose," Christian mumbled.

"Wear this on your shirt." The guard handed him a red triangular patch. "And what is your occupation?"

"I am a clergyman, a church pastor from Stieglitz in the province of Pomerania."

"All you fanatics are in No. 26!"

"26?"

"Yes, you fool, 26! That's the number of your barracks." With a twisted smile he added sarcastically, "Those are our special religious accommodations. We call it the Pastors' Barracks. Now, get out!"

When Christian stepped through the last door, he found that for the first time in weeks he was not in the midst of a herd of humanity. He felt almost as if he were by himself. Yet before him stretched rows and rows of wooden buildings with men walking in every direction. Wide, straight streets ran through the rows of buildings, then abruptly ended before rolls of barbed wire. Next came a wide moat filled with water. On the outer perimeter of the camp were either concrete walls or electrified fences of razor-sharp wire. Each corner was punctuated with a guard tower and mounted machine guns trained on all that was below.

After taking a few steps, Reger stopped to savor the momentary illusion that he was alone. No hand was chained to his wrist or pushing from behind. Everything felt unreal and dreamlike. Possibly none of these indignities had really happened to him. Yet as his hand rubbed across his sore, bare head, the rough stubble sent a sensation through his body that left no doubt about reality.

He took several more steps before realizing that he had no idea of where to go or what to do. Seeing a prisoner with a uniform much dirtier than his own, he asked, "Which way is Barracks No. 26?"

"Up the bunker," the man said, pointing to the north end. Noticing the clean uniform, he added, "The bunker's what we call Main Street. Just keep going down the middle and you'll see 26."

A peculiar, foul odor filled the air. It seemed to come and go as if it were blowing in from somewhere. Certainly the scent was unlike the rotten floor of the train. "Perhaps I am smelling the Dragon's breath today," Christian said aloud as he walked. A passing prisoner stopped as he spoke and stared at him in consternation. Not noticing, Christian continued on his search for No. 26, the Pastors' Barracks. Lonely and apprehensive, he found it and entered.

Two

All of the barracks were exactly the same: wooden, oblong, cracker boxes constructed to be stuffed full of nameless creatures. Inside, the walls were lined with two-decked tiers of cratelike boxes that served as mass beds made to hold 180 people. No. 26 was already filled with 250 men. Clearly, many more would be coming.

When Christian walked down the center aisle of No. 26, he was astonished to discover the many nationalities of the prisoners.

"You are a minister?" he asked doubtfully.

"Oui," a Frenchman answered.

"And you?" he said, turning to another prisoner.

"Ja," a Dutchman answered.

As he looked around, he saw men who appeared to be Czechs, Poles, Italians, Belgians, perhaps even a few Yugoslavs. It was almost as if he were attending some sort of bizarre European convention of poverty-stricken clergymen.

"You are Protestants?" he asked a small, huddled group. "Are all of these men from the Confessing Church?"

"No," a tall, thin man answered. "Many of us are Catholic priests and a few are Greek Orthodox."

"Oh, I see," Christian said, raising his eyebrows. "I have just arrived and do not understand."

"Few people would," a smaller man added. "The SS has done a good job of concealing our existence."

"Let me introduce myself," the tall, thin man offered. "I am Leonard Steinwender. I came here from Buchenwald prison and have been here six months." He had a noble bearing that conveyed good breeding and education. The strong, proud face with intelligent eyes seemed a strange contrast to the dingy, dirty uniform. However, the strength in his voice was reassuring evidence that the past months had not broken his spirit.

"I see," said Christian. He had never been around many Catholics and they made him feel awkward and ill at ease.

"We no longer make distinctions about our different doctrines," Steinwender returned, sensing Reger's uneasiness. "Here we have found that we must all stand together in order to survive."

"I see." Christian immediately realized how distant and professional he sounded.

"My name is Werner Sylten," said the smaller man, extending his hand. "I am a Lutheran pastor and have been here nearly a year." His cheeks were unnaturally shrunken and the grayness in his hair seemed to run into his colorless face. Though his handshake attempted to be firm and hearty, Christian felt a foreboding feebleness in the grip. Obviously, the man was not well.

Christian noticed that he could gauge a man's imprisonment by the length of his hair. To the left was a man whose hair was still quite short.

"And I am August Schmidt, a Catholic priest." The twinkle in his eye seemed very out of place. In fact, his whole face conveyed a warmth that was inviting and comforting. The missing tooth on the left side added a touch of comedy. Instantly, Christian knew he would like this man.

"I am glad to meet you all." Christian felt himself beginning to relax.

"Let us give you your first lesson in life at Dachau," Schmidt began. "In the Pastors' Barracks you are among brothers, but outside you must trust no one else."

"We are in a time when deception reigns supreme," Leonard added.

"Indeed!" Sylten's voice was flat and hard. "Betrayal sent me here. When I was first imprisoned at Frankfurt, I managed to escape. On my way home I decided to stop at a fellow pastor's house. I was hungry and thought he might help me. When I told him of my predicament, he invited me for coffee."

Reger noticed the man's hand began to curl in a fist. Although his voice was without emotion, the taut whiteness of his knuckles spoke quite clearly.

"While I waited for the coffee, this obedient servant of God went into the back room and called the police. He kept me talking while the SS came and surrounded the house."

"Many of us are political prisoners," Leonard further instructed, "but there are also gypsies, criminals, and a number of Jews. You must remember that there are many collaborators who will do anything to save their hides. There are some good capos, but not many."

"Capos?" Christian wondered aloud. "What are capos?"

"Capos are prisoners who have been selected for the marvelous job of overseeing their fellow prisoners," August explained. "The Nazis use this quaint method to try to divide us. Some capos just try to survive and others tend to be a mite brutal. They will test your sense of humor!"

"You must never be late for roll call," Leonard interjected, and drew himself up to his full height with Prussian stiffness, his iron jaw jutting. "Twice a day we line up in Roll Call Square. Everyone must stand at absolute attention regardless of his health or circumstances until every man is accounted for. Regardless of the weather you must stand with your cap off."

"Any error can subject you to a severe beating," Sylten said, pointing his finger in Christian's direction, "and you must not cost the rest of the group by ever keeping them standing outside when the winter has set in."

Christian vigorously nodded his head. As a good German Protestant he had learned that magistrates were God's left hand. Their commands were to be obeyed. For a brief moment the irony of his situation occurred to him. He and the men who surrounded him were all devoted to obeying the law absolutely as a matter of Christian principle. Yet here they were discussing survival in a prison more severe and cruel than any Christian could ever have imagined.

Schmidt lowered his voice and leaned into the group. "There is a rumor that a Catholic bishop from Munich has been put in the special detention cells in the camp jail. They say that the Gestapo arrested Bishop Neuhausler to 'cool him,' as the SS calls it. Also, I heard that Martin Niemöller has been sent here."

"Niemöller!" Reger exclaimed. "I know him. He is one of us. He is a leader in the Confessing Church!"

"I believe they are concentrating all of us in one place," Sylten warned. "It is a bad sign and may mean worse things are ahead."

"Worse?" Christian asked incredulously. "What could be worse than what is here?"

"The answer is blowing through the trees," Steinwender said cynically. "It is in the air."

The entire group laughed nervously.

"What are you saying?" Reger asked. "You speak in riddles."

"Didn't you smell it?" Sylten sounded harsh. "Surely you

noticed when you came in. The smoke blows through constantly."

"Yes, it did bother me but I have never smelled anything like that." Reger was apologetic.

"It's from the crematoriums," Steinwender said flatly.

"The wind periodically blows the smoke from the crematoriums through the camp. The ovens are located next to the far wall."

"What are you saying?"

"My new friend," Sylten said with increasing intensity, "prisoners are being burned up every day of the week in this place. People who die go up the chimneys!"

"They are killing people here?"Christian could barely mouth the words. "People are dying in this place?"

"You have come to a place . . . " Father Schmidt stopped. There was no smile and his eyes narrowed. Then slowly and carefully choosing his words, he continued, "From whence most of us will probably never return."

"This cannot be!" Christian protested. "We all know what the Nazis are, but this is Germany. We are citizens of a civilized nation!"

A coldness fell over the group that left each man feeling isolated, lonely, and silent. Christian searched their faces for a denial. Instead, he found a stony affirmation in each man's eyes.

"Warn him about the infirmary," Sylten started again. "Karl Leisner can tell you best because he has certainly been there. Karl, tell our new prisoner about the hospital."

A frail, worn-looking young man with sunken cheeks crawled from the back of the wooden crates. He wore small, round glasses so thick that his deep-set eyes looked like beady, black dots.

"Karl is a deacon and hopes to be ordained to the priesthood," Sylten explained. "His health is not the best."

"If you must go," Karl said, sitting up, "make sure you get out as quickly as possible but under no circumstances let them certify you for the invalid transports. They will try to tell you that they will take you to another camp where the work is easier."

"And then you will disappear off the face of the earth," Sylten concluded.

"It took us some time to piece the whole story together," Karl specified. "At first shoes, glasses, clothes, and even artificial legs of sick prisoners began to reappear in the camp. One of the capos noticed that those who left on transports were forced to exchange whatever they had for even more inferior shoes or clothes. All items of value were taken away."

"One of the prisoners who worked in the administration office found that the transportation orders were for Hartheim Castle near Linz," another inmate chimed in. "Before the war, the castle had been used as an asylum for the insane."

"Finally the rest of the story was smuggled back to us," Karl said, smiling sadly. "The sick are being gassed to death in that old castle." Pathos and compassion seemed lined in his face as he silently continued nodding yes and shook a bony finger at the astounded and bewildered new prisoner.

"They will assign you a work detail in the fields and you will be taxed to your limits," Sylten picked up the theme again, "but do not use the infirmary as an excuse not to work."

"Thank you." Christian nodded to each of the group. "Thank you for your instruction." As he turned around, he noticed that Wilhelm Dittner had also arrived in the barracks. Perhaps, someone would start explaining things to him.

Three

As Christian peered into the darkness, he could hear the heavy breathing that surrounded him more like a blanket of humidity than of sound. The heat of the summer day was still radiating both from the men and the walls. Fortunately, he had discovered an open knothole in the wall and by placing his face to the opening he could inhale a cooling breeze from outside.

He tried to find some comfort, but lying against uneven pine boards offered no hope of that. For a while he wondered if he could ever learn to sleep with such constant distraction but then he remembered how even that had become possible while being forced to sit up in the boxcar.

How did I get here? he questioned himself. *How did I ever get here?* Scenes of home, church meetings, and friends began to flow through his mind. And at each change of scenery he wondered if he were a fool.

The guardhouse lights flashing outside the barracks reminded him of the first night the Brownshirts had attacked his home eight years ago. The lights of the trucks had beamed into the bedroom windows first. He remembered the sounds of men leaping from their trucks and shouting. Suddenly, shock waves went through the small parsonage as mobs began beating violently on the sides of the trucks and screaming at the top of their lungs.

"Christian, what are they doing?" his wife Mina had asked, clutching at his arm and the bed sheets and trying to hide beneath both.

"I don't know." He tried to lie still and listen. "I can't make out what they are saying."

Then a single cry began to emerge above the babble: "Traitors of Germany! Traitors of Germany! Traitors of Germany!"

Huddling together beneath the covers, Christian and Mina clung together as the roar and the truck lights continued to pierce through their windows. "Oh no!" Mina whispered in his ear. "We are being attacked just as they warned us they would do. Maybe we can escape through the backdoor."

Christian had already begun inching toward the edge of the

bed. Carefully they approached the windows to peer out through the parted curtains. Against the lights of the trucks they saw the silhouettes of party uniforms. Faces were lost in the darkness, but the men looked young and were clearly holding sticks and clubs.

From atop one of the trucks a lone voice began growling, "Clerics and their followers are traitors of our country. Those who don't follow us, we take you out!"

Then the chant began again like a litany of death: *"Wir schlagen sie zusammen!"* "We take you out! We take you out!" Finally the chorus ended and the men began piling back into the trucks.

One last voice shouted, "You have been warned before. You will come into line or worse will happen!"

Now as Christian lay cramped between the hot bodies, he remembered how he and Mina had lain in bed till late in the night wrestling with what might follow. Should they stop holding their meetings of the Confessing Church? Should they stop organizing other groups? Perhaps it would be wiser to give in to this new fanatical patriotism?

In the end, Mina had put her arm across his chest and said, "I am not afraid of anything but losing you. Do not retreat an inch on my account." With that, Christian's fear had turned into anger and indignation.

Perhaps, that's when I should have stopped, he now thought, *but I would have violated everything I had ever stood for. And I had to correct the first impression I left in the church. I couldn't let the people think that I still in any way agreed with the National Socialists.*

He was embarrassed to remember how he had once worn the Brownshirt uniform when Hitler first came to power. But then everyone was doing the same to demonstrate patriotism and his hopes for the future. While Christian had not been enthusiastic about Hitler, he did appear as the only alternative to the Bolsheviks and to the rampant depression devouring the country.

Another face intruded into his reverie. Grell, the provost, and his band of racists appeared. Christian remembered when these "German Christians" had come to a minister's meeting to persuade the group to endorse their stand on Aryan superiority as reflecting God's intentions. He recalled their strange manipulation of words that said one thing and meant another.

"My fellow pastors," Grell began that fall afternoon, "there is some confusion among us about how to relate to this new marvelous opportunity that God has given us in National Socialism and Adolf Hitler. We have come to discuss this matter as we are promoting the wonderful ideas that can bring spiritual revival to our nation."

Christian remembered how appealing the words were. Each promise had touched a yearning in every man there.

"German Christians recognize that there must be an Aryan solidarity on the issues of faith and politics." Grell's voice became more emphatic. "We must not have a divided house or our enemies will triumph! We are only advocating that love of country is part of our faith. In this great hour of hope we must band together to eliminate all enemies to our progress."

The word "eliminate" sent the meeting into a wild and frantic debate. Rzadki, a fellow pastor, furiously attacked the whole German Christian platform. He accused Grell of being an antichrist. "Your words are one heresy hunting another," he shouted at him.

Grell became livid. Many of the pastors were uncertain. And the meeting ended in confusion.

During the ensuing year, a rumor circulated that Rzadki had been taken to a concentration camp at Sachsenhausen, interrogated mercilessly, forced from his church, and banished to East Prussia. Christian remembered how hard it had been for him to believe such reports. *Exaggeration, overreaction,* he had thought to himself when the details were whispered. Even now lying in the midst of a crowded loneliness, he found it hard to comprehend that people who called themselves Christians had contributed to persecution and imprisonment of fellow churchmen and, of course, himself.

Finally, as was always the case, Mina's was the last face to return. He had found that his mind could become a motion-picture projector that would play her face over and over again in his memory. He tried to bring back their times together as if replaying them might let him once more crawl back into the scene.

She was lovely. Oh, yes, she was more than lovely. Her face was softly rounded and her light-blue eyes seemed always to comprehend more than was being said. She had a gift of sensitivity.

Mina's blond hair framed her face with just the right touch of femininity. That special womanly quality extended to the taper of her graceful fingers that were so adept at the keyboard. Indeed, her melodies that poured from the piano had always fulfilled Christian's own love for music. They had spent hours together as he played the violin or sang while she accompanied him.

Always proper, she had never been one given to special allurements. Yet even with high-necked dresses and hair pulled back in a tight bun, Mina radiated a unique beauty filled with goodness and kindness.

One of their little songs seemed to be almost audible. In memory, he could see her fingers run up and down the piano keys. With the introductory notes finished, she would nod her head and he would begin in his tenor voice. A sound almost escaped from his lips and he had to restrain from humming.

Mina Rothenhofer had been the only woman in his life. His family's meager income and his own resources had been strained to the limits completing his education. There had been no time or money for a social life. In fact, if she had not been a parishioner in his first church, they would probably have always remained at a distance from each other.

Again he almost chuckled aloud as he remembered how he had used every excuse a pastor could have for visiting her house. In the Protestant parish of Hockenheim, a schoolteacher was always an excellent prospect for volunteer service. How he had worked that opportunity!

Formality and propriety had been essential. Custom dictated a distance that placed the vicar on a lofty and socially difficult pedestal. Yet their companionship had satisfied a hunger that Christian had not even known existed within himself.

Hockenheim had been innundated with the same economic disaster that had befallen all of Germany. Each day unemployed people clamored after bread and talked of radical political solutions. In that cold winter of uncertainty, she had become for him a springtime of warmth, grace, and abundance.

"Mina, I want to marry you." He remembered how the words had come out so suddenly, so bluntly, so clumsily. He had no idea how to say such things.

"O Christian," her voice had been so warm, yet pained, "this cannot be. The villagers will talk. They will gossip that I am much too old for you. I am expected to become the spinster schoolteacher of the village. I can only bring you trouble."

"I don't care," he replied, surprised at his growing forcefulness and sense of control. "I don't care, Mina. I only want you."

"O Christian, I do love you." Her sensitive eyes had probed his face for any hint of reservation that might be there. Then she had answered, "I would be honored to be your wife."

With the simplicity of those words their lives began blending together. On that night they had embraced for the first time.

As she had predicted, a storm of gossip surrounded their quiet, simple wedding. The Hockenheim parish was a small place in a world in which unusual events seldom happened. People who have little to do are easily preoccupied with little things. Their romance was quickly blown out of proportion by village busybodies.

So, in a few months they were on their way to Pomerania and the village of Stieglitz. They could not have realized that the uproar in Hockenheim would be nothing compared to the turmoil they would find in their new parish. But in those following years she had stood in the midst of all the threats like a tower of steel. Mina had never ceased to be his source of consolation.

Once more the matchbox came to mind. Even in that special intervention of God, Mina's words had strengthened, encouraged, and sustained him. The message of faith he had found inside the box again insisted he could live through this time of extreme testing.

Then August Schmidt's words of the afternoon began their haunting work. " . . . Most of us will probably never return." As the afternoon had unfolded, Christian had to fight back a creeping terror that now seemed even closer in the darkness of the barracks. Every resource of memory, love, and faith would be required to endure.

At last his thoughts fused into a prayer that merged with drowsiness and then restless sleep.

He had finished his first day at Dachau.

CHAPTER THREE   △
THE DEVIL'S WORK—1940

One

"PSST, HOW LONG have you been here?" the short man next to him whispered coarsely.

Carefully holding his place in the roll call line, No. 26 661 turned to observe the white-skulled prisoner clad in a clean uniform. Almost instinctively he ran his hand through his own chopped, brown hair and was amazed at how long it had become. No. 26 661? For a moment he stumbled over his own name and realized that somewhere in the past weeks he had lost a piece of his humanity.

"A long time," he at last answered, trying to sound disinterested. However, to his surprise, he could not recall how many weeks or days it had been. He puzzled over the answer for a moment before the panic finally gripped him. He had truly lost track of the weeks! Time had blurred together and days had lost any distinctiveness. All he could remember was the endless work from dawn to dusk, and now the sun was just about to rise again.

"Attention! Caps off!" echoed down the rows behind him. Instantly his body became erect as he snatched the cap from his head.

When he had first arrived, the heat of summer was almost unbearable. Now it was much cooler and the mornings were almost crisp. "Surely it had to be September," he calculated.

"Keep the rows straight or you will be here until the snow blows." Somebody somewhere was in trouble. He stiffened.

No. 26 661 knew well how incredibly severe the consequences could be if the roll call was not met with absolute punctuality and precision. Regardless of health or circumstances, each man had better stand motionless and straight until every prisoner was accounted for or else face severe punishment.

The count seemed to wear on endlessly as threats and accusations rang through the morning chill. Christian tried to focus his thoughts as he pondered his lapse of memory. As usual, he had been up since 4 A.M. The 6 A.M. roll call was only a pause before the day of grueling work that would continue until 8:30 that night. Nothing made this day any different from any other. *Still,* he agonized, *I must remember exactly how long I have been here.*

"Some have not yet learned the lessons of Dachau," the voice boomed over the loudspeaker. "We remind you of the penalty to be paid by those who will not cooperate."

From behind the rows of prisoners a group of naked men, cowering between guards with clubs and sticks, was marched to the front of the assembly. The soldiers whipped and swatted at the men as the procession took center stage, and the result was a bizarre, comic dance, a performance the guards obviously enjoyed.

As the prisoners stood trying to cover themselves, the loudspeaker listed charges of "slacking in the fields," "trying to escape work," and "unconstructive attitudes," as the guards struck the men until, one by one, each was prostrate on the ground.

The first time No. 26 661 had witnessed one of these spectacles he felt as if he would bolt from the line. Now he maintained a stony stare, fastening his vision on a tree-lined ridge far beyond the fence. But there was no way he could erase the memory of that first horror show when he had seen two men beaten to death for trying to escape.

"To show our mercy," the loudspeaker explained, "these examples will now be taken by invalid transports to other camps for new assignments."

Shuddering at the thought, No. 26 661 took one last look at the men on the ground to see if he might identify any of them. Although none was familiar, he was not surprised to see that they looked distinctly Jewish.

"Assemble now for your work details," the loudspeaker instructed. "Remember, work makes you free!"

The lines of prisoners relaxed and the men began to shuffle in various directions. To his left, No. 26 661 recognized one of the pastors from the Confessing Church. He turned and walked casually toward the fellow prisoner.

"Niemöller?" he queried inconspicuously. "Have you seen or heard of Martin Niemöller?"

The man seemed to not hear. Though he paused, his eyes looked straight ahead. Then he spoke in a stage whisper. "Ya, Niemöller is here. They are keeping him in a special cell near the Jourhaus."

The two men then shuffled on in opposite directions.

It would be impossible for me to ever see him, No. 26 661 thought to himself. *Certainly it would be foolish to try.*

He had almost completely dismissed the thought when it occurred to him how quickly his mind had dropped the idea. Though he was by nature concerned with the welfare of other people, that sensitivity seemed to be slipping away. Earlier he hadn't even cared to answer the new prisoner in line next to him. In fact, taking care of himself had become his only interest. As he walked into the midst of his work company, he looked around at his fellow clergymen and wondered if they had the same feelings.

Men nodded to one another as they formed the lines in which they would march out to the fields. Each was quietly steeling himself for the day that lay ahead. No. 26 661 found his usual place and stared aimlessly into space.

"We must not lose ourselves," an elderly man said to him. "Today, Reger, we must still care." Hearing his name immediately felt reassuring and humanizing.

"Ya," he replied, "that is certainly true."

Fritz Seitz had been the first German Catholic priest to be sentenced to Dachau. Each day they marched out together. His unexpected admonition surprised Christian, but also gave him special encouragement.

"Begin!" the captain shouted to the group. "A rousing song should prepare us. Let us go forth to our glorious work singing the songs of our nation." The captain clicked his heels and roared the "*Seig Heil!*" Nazi salute.

The guards' patriotic chorus started the group marching in place, and the men picked up the tune and the tempo as they tramped out under the gate and toward the fields. Each morning and night they were greeted with the same lie: "Work Makes You Free."

The "glorious work" shared by No. 26 661 and his comrades was the maintenance of the herb fields. The SS kept an enormous plantation of medicinal and spice plants just beyond the camp's barbed-wire fences. The impressive, meticulously kept rows were cultivated at a high cost to the prisoners, for regardless of the fierceness of the South Bavarian winds and weather, these fields were worked seven days a week.

When the men came to the edge of the fields, the threats and harassment began again. "We have no time to waste," echoed even from the capos. "Come on, you pigs, into the trenches. Faster! Hurry!"

44

No. 26 661 inhaled deeply, knowing well there would be no slack time until evening. The rules of the field did not allow breaks.

"I will try not to lose myself today," Fritz said, smiling at him.

"But let us not disappear either," No. 26 661 warned, motioning toward the chimneys.

"Now that it is cooler, the midday will be more bearable."

"For you, it will be," No. 26 661 answered, "but the weather makes little difference when I am carrying the buckets."

"Begin!" echoed across the field. The two men nodded to each other and went their separate ways.

That morning seemed to move fairly quickly and for some reason Christian didn't feel as physically empty as usual. But as the sun rose higher, he felt the dread rising in him. Noontime was the worst of all.

"All right, No. 26 661, start getting the buckets out." The capo dipped his ladle into the boiling caldron and poured the steaming mush into the buckets at Reger's feet. "And if you spill any, you know what the rest of the inmates will do!"

The metal handles always cut into Christian's hands, increasing his fear that he would stumble and drop the buckets. Of course, if he did, many prisoners would be left without even the meager gruel. Such a mistake might eventually cost him his life.

With the enormous buckets in each hand, he strained forward, carefully stepping between the rows and trying to foresee any holes in the ground. The steam seemed to crawl up his arms and he felt his own sweat making the handles even more slippery. His only pause would come as the men cleaned out the buckets. Their hunger was such that the pails seemed to drain themselves in a matter of seconds.

"Hurry up!" the capo snarled. "Other men are waiting. Your slowness costs us rest time."

Quickly, No. 26 661 snatched the buckets and started back to the black caldron. Back and forth he went across the field until every man had received the tasteless meal. More palatable to pigs, it was still their only life and, therefore, always silently and feverishly received.

Two

When noontime passed, No. 26 661 was sent to another task. Today the extra men were moving dirt back and forth across the field.

"Let the lunchman push the wheelbarrow now," one of the guards ordered, sneering at the crew. "He's had a nice rest. Let him take it a couple of turns."

Christian's back muscles strained and wrenched as he started to push the cart forward. At least the weight didn't seem to cut into the palms of his hands. Up and down he traveled once, then a second time.

"Here! Stop this slack," a guard demanded of one of the prisoners holding a shovel. "Don't waste time! Get this thing full!"

Immediately, more dirt was piled on top of the already full wheelbarrow. Christian wasn't sure he could even push it, but somehow, someway, the wheel began to turn and he struggled off to the opposite corner of the field to dump it. Immediately, he went back for the next load.

Back and forth. Back and forth. Back and forth the wheelbarrow cut through the furrows and wound down the path. Sometimes he got away with a small load, but most of the time the cart was filled to overflowing. Even when the sun had begun to travel toward the horizon, the pace did not slacken. Back and forth. Back and forth. Back and forth.

If it had not been for his unusual athletic build, Christian probably would have cracked that day The years he had spent as a youth working out in the school gymnasium were his salvation. The parallel bars, the Roman rings, the exercises had built an endurance into his back and shoulders that was the envy of his schoolmates. The residue of that strength was all that held him together now.

Near the end of the afternoon, he tried to distract himself and make his mind forget about his body. Only then did he reflect on the assignment. Dirt from one place was being taken to another. There was no purpose, no reason, no meaning to the task. The endless trips with the wheelbarrow were a marching in place, a marking time, an exercise in futility.

"Tomorrow you can move the dirt back to where we began," the guard announced to the group. No. 26 661 put down the empty wheelbarrow and straightened up. His back felt as though another move would break it in two. "These exercises will help you learn the value of obedience. Eventually you will get your priorities straight," the guard declared, his voice laden with condescension.

No. 26 661 glanced at the other men. The degradation of their situation no longer seemed to register with them. Perhaps they lacked the strength to care. With exhaustion and anticipation, each eyed the end of the field where the sun was falling.

When the whistle blew, the prisoners mechanically shuffled together into a unit for their return. The pace even picked up as they tramped down the road. The wind had increased somewhat and the smoke drifted out to meet them as they approached the gate. *The aroma of death is still everywhere,* he thought to himself. *It is in what we do, how we do it, and what is done to us. Smoke seems to cloud what we think, believe, and hope.* Then he lost his train of thought. Once again, an all-pervasive loneliness engulfed him as he marched along in the cluster of men that blended into the assembly on Roll Call Square. The 8:30 head count and harangue was about to commence.

Standing in line did not expend much energy, yet there was no relief either. Another typical day had slipped past. Defeat, defilement, and despair was its only profit. The pollution from the skies seemed to have seeped through his nostrils and into his soul. He no longer wanted to try, or perhaps, to survive.

From somewhere within, a new and unexpected thought arose. Maybe today there would be a letter for him. While it was a remote possibility, the thought alone offered solace. Might it be?

Yet he knew he must sit down or stretch out on the ground to recover any vestige of energy that might be scavenged for the rest of the day. When the dismissal was sounded, he sank in a heap. The others almost escaped into sleep, but he fought back drowsiness for fear that he would lose a grip on time and sleep through the supper hour. His muscles were already getting stiff and he knew how important it was to keep moving. With more resolution than reserve, he started toward the mail office.

At the edge of the bunker, a small crowd was standing in front of the infirmary. Two guards came out the door carrying the limp body of a prisoner. Though he was obviously dead, his clothes were strangely soaked and dripping. As the men shuffled past with the body, the SS guard in charge pronounced indifferently, "Heart attack."

"He was a Jew," Auboiroux, the Communist, whispered to Christian as they disappeared around the corner. Responsible for brushing door latches throughout the camp with disinfectant, Auboiroux was known by everyone to be a good source of information.

"A Jew?" No. 26 661 asked in consternation.

Ignoring his question, the Communist added, "The man did not die of heart problems. They killed him."

"Killed him?"

"Of course! The block leader had them take him into the washroom." The Communist lowered his voice even more. "They held him against the wall and sprayed cold water around his heart until it failed. That's why he is so wet."

"My God!" No. 26 661 exhaled.

"There is no God." The Communist walked back into the infirmary.

The scene dissolved before Christian's eyes like a grotesque dream. Had he really seen two guards and a dead Jew? Was his tired mind deceiving him? Yet he did know Auboiroux, the French Communist. He trudged on to the mail office.

To his astonishment, a letter *was* waiting! The whole group crowded around to savor any morsel of contact from the outside world. Dittner was always busy about the mail office and elbowed his way to Christian's side.

"Who is it from?" Dittner asked feverishly.

"Just a minute." No. 26 661 motioned the crowd back. "Give me some breathing room."

"Every bit of news can be vital," Dittner insisted.

"It is from my wife," he said hopefully. "I'm sure it is." Ripping open the envelope, he found his dreams confirmed.

"Is there word about how the war is going?" a voice implored.

"Has she been harassed?" someone else asked.

"Please, please!" Christian begged, waving the letter exasperatedly. "I can't even read with your incessant questions. You know that anything of any real significance would have been censored. Please give me a moment."

The group became quiet as he carefully, slowly devoured every sentence, every phrase, every word. Finally he sighed. "My wife writes that since they have stopped my salary she must find some other source of income."

"What will she do?" A man grasped at his sleeve. "How will she survive?"

No. 26 661 studied the man's face for a second. The question was really about the other prisoner's wife. How would any of their wives live?

"She writes that she thinks she has found a job as an organist. She says it is not much, but she believes it will carry her through. My wife is a very talented person."

"Good!"

"Excellent!"

"Also she writes she is doing her best to keep our church together during my absence. Many of the people have forsaken us for fear of reprisal, but a faithful core still remains."

"That is an encouragement!" said one of the men, nodding and smiling.

Someone else received a letter and immediately the group turned its attention to the next piece of mail. Again they clamored like hungry children at mealtime. All moved on except Dittner, who pulled away from the mail office and followed Christian.

"I have an important message for you," Dittner said, looking in all directions to make sure no one was standing too close. "Contact has been made with the outside."

"How can that be?"

"A few prisoners who have been released have helped establish this link," he explained as they strolled back down the bunker. "They were all threatened with immediate arrest and return if they spoke of what they saw here. Of course, return would mean quick death."

No. 26 661 nodded, remembering the special patches given to returnees. He had seen the work details *they* received.

"Nevertheless," Dittner continued, "they are helping the best way they know. They have helped smuggle a few radio receivers into the camp. We will be able to know about the outside."

"Wonderful!" Christian exploded, then grasped his mouth for fear the outburst would be heard.

"Perhaps your letters will help get a bit of information through someday."

"Of course, of course."

"I will let you know, but tell no one."

"I will see you at the barracks," No. 26 661 affirmed, walking off in the opposite direction to appear that the contact had no significance.

He would not tell Dittner, but he seriously questioned whether he would involve Mina in any schemes to convey clandestine information. Now that he understood the consequences, he would do nothing which might send her to a place like Dachau. *Surely there is a limit to what one can do,* he thought to himself. *There must be a line somewhere that one does not cross. I wonder where that line is?*

The whole issue confused him. Obviously, Mina had intended to be a part of this stand against evil, and they *had* stood together. Yet would they have done all of those things if they had really known the consequences? He couldn't decide what they would have done if they had realized how diabolical the Nazis really were. His motivations seemed unclear, undefined, and confused. Naiveté, courage, and prudence melted together into a mental blur.

Three

"Come in, my friend!" Fritz called, as Christian approached the doorway of No. 26. "Come in and be a human being again."

"Christian is back," Leonard Steinwender echoed through the crowded barracks. "He is all right."

"We missed you at the service," Werner greeted him, "and were concerned something might have happened. The worship was deeply inspiring. We were lifted by it."

He truly smiled for the first time that day. "I was delayed. I had a letter from my wife and read it very slowly."

"Oh, of course."

"How wonderful."

"An answered prayer in itself!"

The little group sat down together to assess their day. The few moments of reflection each evening sustained and nourished them emotionally. Each man leaned eagerly forward. Leonard and Fritz sat on the edge of the wooden beds and Christian and Werner on the floor. Heinrich Gruber walked over and leaned against the crates. Gruber had only recently joined the inner circle of Christian's friends. Though his plain, round face looked rather peasantlike, Heinrich had an unusually sharp mind. When he began to speak, he stood out in any group. Such ability had earned him a free trip to Dachau.

"We have survived another one," August Schmidt declared, poking his head over the top of the wooden rack. "Another glorious, typical day is done." His impish grin and ironic jokes were always reassuring.

"I'm not sure of the month." Christian frowned.

"It is October," Dittner answered as he emerged from a cluster of men in front of them. "Today is October 24. In another month the snow will start to pile."

His answer gave Christian an immediate sense of relief.

"Why do you think they have allowed us to build the little chapel area in front of our barracks?" Heinrich asked. "In the midst of all the persecution, this seems like a strange privilege."

"I overheard the SS say it was a concession to the priests," Dittner replied, squatting down. "They said it was the result of official pressure."

"I'm sure the Vatican pressured them," Leonard added. "They know what's happening to us priests."

"We are surrounded by ironies." Dittner chuckled cynically. "On the other hand, you Catholics have suffered ten times what we Protestants have at the hands of National Socialism."

"Oh, there has been plenty for all of us," Leonard countered. "I was imprisoned first at Buchenwald where I saw a Protestant

52

die a tragic death. His name was Paul Schneider."

"You knew Paul?" Christian was animated. "He has been one of the key leaders of the Confessing Church!"

"His courage was unbelievable!" Leonard stared intensely at the group. "In the camp he would not salute the swastika flag so they put him in a special torture cell that overlooked the assembly area. When the prisoners would line up for roll call, he would shout out the window, 'Jesus says, "I am the resurrection and the life." ' Immediately, the guards would descend on him and beat him into silence. We could hear the blows clear out in the yard."

Christian inched forward, his face unable to mask his shock. "How did he endure?"

"On occasions when the SS camp leader was reviewing the prisoners, Paul would shout, 'You are a murderer! I accuse you publicly before God's tribunal of massacre.' Then he would start to name prisoners who had recently died. The beatings that followed were inhuman."

"How long did he last?" Fritz asked.

"For thirteen months he kept at it. Then one morning in the spring, after the guards left, no sound ever came from the cell again."

Christian bit the side of his finger and tried to control his emotions.

"As I said," Leonard concluded, "we have all paid our price, but he was a true saint."

"What is it we are fighting for?" Christian suddenly shouted angrily. "What are we fighting? Sometimes I'm not sure. Are we battling over politics? Are we fighting for truth? Is it all worth the death of one man like Paul Schneider?"

"Have you forgotten our motto?" Dittner snapped back. "What has been the battle cry that the Confessing Church has sounded?"

"You mean the quotation you use from Hebrews?" a priest

asked. "Isn't it something like, 'We are not among those who shrink back and are lost; we have the faith to make life our own'?"

"Exactly!" Dittner sounded bitter and hard. "We are in a spiritual battle that cuts across every line—political, national, religious, and personal. These are external issues!"

The group was silent, but listened intensely as Gruber stood up like a preacher mounting his pulpit. His blue eyes flashed.

"In 1932 when I was studying the Book of Revelation, I saw the truth. There is a trinity of evil that is loose in this world and no one avoids the conflict. The embodiment and source of all that is diabolical, corrupting, and painful is the ancient Dragon that seeks to work his will by riding into our midst on the back of the great Beast. The Beast is the biblical symbol for corrupted governments that yield themselves to his will. When I understood that, I knew Hitler, National Socialism, the SS, the Brownshirts, all of these were manifestations of that Beast!"

"And the third part of that trinity is counterfeit religion," Heinrich Gruber continued. "Nazism is a religion—a vicious, devouring religion! That's why they attack the Jews, us, everything that is holy!"

"Isn't it strange," Christian pondered, "how none of us saw this in the beginning?"

"That's true!" Leonard gestured vigorously. "Remember how we talked of Nazism and National Socialism as being a 'German sunrise'? I remember many theologians at the university speaking of a great spiritual revival that Hitler would bring to the country."

"Although it's very painful to admit," Christian confessed, "I even bought a Brownshirt uniform in '32. The parishioners applauded it and I even wore it in the pulpit."

"Certainly!" another Protestant chimed in. "Many of us felt that wearing the uniform was simply the patriotic thing to do."

"I mean nothing personal," Gruber interrupted, patting

Christian's arm, "but you Protestants lost your direction much earlier than '32. You became man-centered instead of God-centered. Many of your leaders could not see the religious implications of what Hitler proclaimed."

"And that is why you opened your office to protect Jews in Berlin!" Christian had sudden insight. "That is why you started your work to help persecuted Jews!"

"My concern was humanitarian," Heinrich added, "but the issues were also particularly religious and that is why I felt no regret when the SS arrested me."

"Oh, you are so right!" Christian was becoming more excited. "My wife and I finally saw this religious side of Nazism in 1933. We happened onto a group of Brownshirts out in the woods near our church. They had spread a swastika flag over a tree stump to make an altar. A young father held up his baby and recited a pledge to die for Germany. He said, 'I believe in the deaths of those who die for the people because my god is my people.' Then they baptized the baby 'in the name of the Father-land and to the glory of Germany.' After that experience, I knew there would be no sunrise."

"Remember what they did to Fritz?" August continued. "He was the first German Catholic priest to be sent here. Tell them why they sentenced you."

"You won't believe this," Seitz explained. "I am at Dachau merely for hearing the confession of a Polish citizen. Can you imagine?

"But nothing compares with my humiliation on that first day here. When I came through the gates, an SS guard pulled my rosary from my pocket and hung it around my head so that the crucifix dangled on my forehead. He drove me around the assembly ground screaming, 'The first pig from the Old Reich has arrived!' When I fell down, he kept screaming that after the war all priests would be locked up and the Catholic swindle would be over"

"That is not the worst part." August prompted him.

"When they found my picture of the Virgin Mary they told jokes about her virginity so vulgar that I can't even repeat them."

"These devils must be annihilated," Dittner shouted, and then immediately lowered his voice lest a capo hear him. "This is a battle to the death. The Cross is the great sword by which we must smite this enemy. We must strike them in God's name!"

"No! No!" Leonard corrected him. "That was not the way Paul Schneider fought. And we will remember him long after we have forgotten the warriors who spilled blood with the sword."

"And he is dead." Dittner's voice was angry and hard.

"But his courage is an example that cannot be killed," Fritz insisted. "In the end, his witness and his faith will be the ultimate victory."

"In our battle we must be different from them," Heinrich lectured Dittner. "If we fight evil in the same way, have we not actually joined the other side?"

"Do you know why I am here?" Werner Sylten asked. "I am a Protestant pastor, but my mother had a Jewish grandmother. Can you imagine? Because of some distant ancestor, I am a candidate for death. If I am to die, I want to have stood for something more than simply hating."

"There are Communists here who are brave men." Christian's voice was uncertain and seemed to be searching to find the way. "And there are Nazis who are more than willing to die for their cause. Surely we are in some way different from them."

"If courage is only putting convictions ahead of survival," Leonard commented, "then we are all the same. Dittner, you suggest nothing more than another alternative in a world of passionate ideas. Does that really make us any better?"

"But we must be responsible." Dittner seemed unmoved by what he had heard. "There is no integrity unless we uphold our sacred obligations."

"So, the Communist believes in his obligations to the workers and the Nazi believes that Aryan purity is sacred," Christian concluded, "and you want us to kill for Jesus' sake."

"Paul Schneider was different from you," Leonard said quietly. Because he was taller than Dittner, he needed only to look down on him for the intensity to be felt. "Surely he believed in the truth, but his faithfulness was much larger than doing his duty. His ultimate commitment was to the love he found revealed in Jesus Christ. In the name of that love, he gave life rather than taking it."

"It is not enough to passionately believe in some ideology!" Werner hammered away at them. "The world is sick from doctrines and creeds. Nobody's completely right! We're all egotists. If we don't have a love that is greater than ourselves, it all turns sour and putrid."

"The Nazis have taught me something very important." Heinrich now got to his feet. His face was flushed, his bulbous nose fiery red. "I have learned that they believe they are entirely and completely right. There is no place for any doubt in their minds. You know why? They must be absolutely correct to justify anything that they do. Every fanatic takes his little piece of the truth and tries to make it the whole for the rest of the world." He paused and pointed harshly at Dittner for a moment. "We must be humble even about the things for which we are willing to die."

"I think," Christian said, trying to sound reconciliatory, "true courage is larger than mere obedience to the truth. I think it is also expressed in those times when we venture beyond ourselves without any certainty that we are truly right."

"I don't know very much about courage," Heinrich grunted. "I only know that I must trust God to help me live in the best way that I can. I do not worry much about dying. Living honestly seems to occupy most of my attention."

Suddenly the lights went out and men began to scramble in all

57

directions. In the darkness, the discussion group was over as men groped to find places to sleep. To his surprise, Christian found he had ended up next to Dittner.

"Let the theologians think what they will," he complained to Christian. "I am going to fight my way out of this place. I will survive and there will be a day of reckoning."

Christian said nothing, only stared into the blackness. At least he now knew how long he had been in the camp. This night Paul Schneider's face came back to him. He tried to picture Paul yelling from the cell window and not retreating in the face of the beatings. He wondered what it all had meant, what difference Paul had made. Could any man fight the Dragon and survive? Or was that even the issue?

Like all of the other nights, his fatigue quickly overwhelmed the soreness in his shoulders and back. Almost immediately, he ceased to feel the hardness of the boards and the crowdedness of the rack.

CHAPTER FOUR △
TO SURVIVE—
1940-41

One

BITTER, COLD WINDS from the Bavarian Alps had already dumped an unusually large amount of snow for so early in the winter. Running up the nearly deserted bunker, two men tried to leap over the small drifts to keep snow from filling their clogs. Still, they were able to maintain their conversation.

"Why *did* you say yes?" Christian asked Dittner, quickly shutting the barracks door behind them as they entered. Each knew that any loss of heat from No. 26 would cost everyone dearly.

"Why does anyone say yes in any difficult matter?" Wilhelm Dittner stomped his feet to awaken the blood from hibernation.

"You could have avoided any involvement against the Nazis," Christian pursued, rubbing his hands together as vigorously as he could. Whatever the effects of the summer heat, nothing hurt like the pain of the freezing ice. "Even in Hesse when you were organizing groups into Confessing Churches, you went out of your way to attack them."

"I cannot tolerate injustice!" Dittner sneered, beating his hands together. "In school I also went out of my way to bully the bullies! Something within me turns to rage when people are being pushed around."

"So, you *were* angry!"

"Well," Dittner half-admitted as he crossed his arms and tucked his hands under his armpits, "I think of the matter as being much larger than anger. Perhaps righteous indignation is a better term."

"Hmmm." Christian studied his friend.

"Have you seen Werner Sylten?" Steinwender burst in through the door. "We can't locate him."

Both men shook their heads.

"Perhaps you don't like being pushed around," Christian decided aloud.

"Of course not!" Dittner snapped. "Does anybody? I hate people who make others feel small or helpless. Is there something wrong with that?"

"Oh, no," Christian insisted, "not at all. I'm only trying to understand your thoughts."

"Listen, Reger, evil is to be fought at all costs with all of our resources. If we don't fight it, we'll be overcome. The worst evil is the official kind, the big, all-encompassing variety that wears uniforms and can render you helpless."

"Is Sylten here?" Another prisoner interrupted the conversation. "Have you seen him?"

"No."

"I haven't seen him for two days," Dittner added.

"So, the strong stands that you take," Christian continued and began to blow' on his hands, "are really prompted by resentment?"

Absolutely!" The blue eyes sparked. "My old man used to terrorize me and my sister, stomping around just like the SS do. I can still hear him screaming and shouting to try to make us cower at his feet. His tirades turned her into a craven puppy that whines and runs from everything. But not me! I will not slink or crawl away from anyone!"

Other prisoners began pouring into the barracks and both men eyed the opening and closing door with offense. The only good thing was that the rapid increase of bodies might ultimately raise the temperature.

"Sylten?" a third prisoner questioned, tugging at Dittner's sleeve. "Have you seen Werner Sylten?"

"No," Dittner snapped. "I haven't seen the man! Shut the door!"

"You know that if they find the radios, they will probably execute you."

"Kill *me?*" Dittner sneered. "You think that they might not just as easily kill *you* for nothing?

"Listen," Dittner lectured and shook his finger in Reger's face, "the trouble with you and most of the rest of Germany is that you don't think. You're like a race of robots that jump every time some official snaps his fingers. You never ask if the man in the uniform might be corrupt and worthless or if he has only come to prostitute your obedience."

"That's not fair!" Christian bristled and his eyes narrowed. "You know the Bible teaches that we are to obey *all* the authorities. From childhood, we have always been taught that God gives us the judges, the officials, the rulers, as a defense against evil men."

"And you have no defense when they turn out to be the very devil!" Dittner poked him in the chest with his finger. "Seven years ago any half-wit should have been able to see where Hitler was going. Don't blame your blindness on the Bible!"

Feeling defensive and confronted, yet not wanting to agree, Christian still wasn't sure how to answer. Pensively, he acknowledged, "I did hear Hitler speak once."

"Oh, really?" Dittner raised his eyebrows in surprise. "When?"

"I was in seminary at Bethel when the National Socialists held a rally in the city hall at Erlangen. That must have been about 1928 or '29. Somewhere around then."

"And you were impressed like the rest?"

"Not in the way you think." Christian was rapidly becoming annoyed. "Sure, Hitler was compelling. What else would he have been otherwise? He screamed; he threatened; his whole speech was a performance in fury. Yet I was more impressed with the effect that his uniformed troops, the swastika flags, and the frenzied salutes had on the crowd. In the end they were on their feet screaming for Germany's freedom, *"Deutschland erwache!"*

"So, what's your point?" Dittner's air of superiority was stifling and repulsive.

"Simply this! The Erlangen town hall was filled with frantic men who were out of work and who saw no hope in the government. Since I was not hungry that day, Hitler didn't impress me very much. But I remembered just a few years earlier when my mother cried herself to sleep because all her inflated money would not buy one loaf of bread!"

Suddenly Christian was shouting and his body was shaking. "So don't sound so omnipotent and omniscient around me! Being right and prudent is not such an easy task in desperate times!"

The exchange had become so heated that it was drawing attention. When the men around them grew silent and started staring, Christian stopped and abruptly walked away. He felt like smashing Dittner in the face. Taking three steps, he halted, turned, and clenched his fists.

"I've found him! I know where he is!" A piercing voice interrupted the steady buzz of conversation throughout the barracks. Pushing and shoving his way through the crowd,

Gruber kept shouting. "Help! Somebody has got to help! I know where Werner is!"

Grabbing him by the arm as he passed by, Dittner demanded, "What's going on here? What are you talking about?"

"They put Sylten in the infirmary. That's why we couldn't find him."

"So what?"

"They won't let him out. That's what!"

"All right, all right," another prisoner joined in, motioning for calm. "So they've got him quarantined or something. He hasn't been gone that long."

"Listen," Gruber still fairly shouted and shook his arm free from Dittner, "they are getting ready to send out another invalid transport to Linz. Don't you get the point? They put Werner in there because of his Jewish background. Whether he's sick or not, they'll load him on that truck and he'll disappear just like the rest."

"Let's go!" Christian announced and darted from across the room. "We have no time."

The three men bolted through the door and began to race up the bunker. The snow had started to blow again and they quickly realized that the barracks was really much warmer than they had thought.

"Not too fast," Dittner warned. "They may think we're trying to escape. Just trot."

"We must get there and back before they turn out the lights," Heinrich puffed. "If they catch us running around after curfew, they might make us stand outside all night." Feeling the bite of the cold, he wheezed, "We don't have much time. Hurry!"

"What can we do?" Christian's words turned into steam. "We need some idea of what to say when we get there."

"Perhaps we can get some other name put on the transport list," Dittner ventured. "Maybe we can bribe a capo to change his roster."

"Bribe?" Gruber panted. "With what?"

"Maybe," Christian thought aloud, "just maybe we could get them to use the name of someone who has already left earlier to fill their count. Perhaps all they need today is a quota."

As the snow cleared slightly and the light of the infirmary appeared just ahead, they realized it looked totally dark inside. As the men stopped abruptly before the door, an eerie silence surrounded them. Sound of movement ought to be coming from the usually crowded building.

Dittner peered into a window and searched for some clue. "Every bed is empty. I can't see anything in there."

Christian jumped up the stairs and barged through the door into the darkness.

"Hey! What's going on?" came from the nearest corner. "What are you doing in here?"

"Where are the patients?" Reger demanded.

"Who are you?" shot back from the blackness.

"Who are you?"

"No. 18 643. Are you a guard?"

"No, I'm a prisoner," Christian snarled. "And I want to know where they've gone!"

"Listen," the surly voice volleyed, "I'm the capo that works here and if you don't get out of here I will call for the guard. Don't come in here acting like you run this hellhole!"

"Please," Christian pleaded, changing his whole tone. "I'm not looking for trouble. I'm just trying to find a friend who disappeared. We know he came here."

"Don't stick your nose where it doesn't belong and you might keep it on your face."

By now his eyes had completely adjusted to the darkness and Christian could see the room was indeed completely empty. The voice in the corner was the only person he could discern in the entire barracks.

"Look," he asked as kindly as he could, "just tell me if they have sent another transport to Linz."

"All I'm saying is that they cleaned house two hours ago and everybody in here was loaded up."

"But have the trucks left?"

"Listen, if you want to get a truck ride, you just stay around here and keep asking questions. Yes, the trucks left! I saw their lights go out the gates. Now that's it! Get out of here!"

Mechanically, Christian backed out. As he shut the door, his hand stayed on the knob while he automatically reached with the other hand as if he might push the door open again. Everything within him insisted that he ought to be able to walk in once more and this time the room would be filled with people and that somewhere Werner Sylten would be lying in a bed.

"They're all gone," he whispered.

"Oh no!" Gruber groaned. "Werner is gone."

"Ya," Dittner concluded bitterly, "Werner is *gone*."

Each man stood rigid in his place, staring straight ahead. Finally, Gruber began to pray, "Out of the depths I cry unto Thee, O Lord. Lord, hear my voice. Let Thy ears be attentive to the voice of my supplication that I make for Werner Sylten and each man that left today."

"Amen," Christian at last mumbled.

Dittner said nothing as the three men turned back to the barracks. His face was set like a rock, his jaw locked.

The biting wind no longer seemed to matter.

Two

The loudspeaker continued to pour out its vilification and demands as each man stood erect and face forward. The roll call assembly was no place for deviation. Still, No. 26 661 could carefully study Herman Metz in the row just in front of him.

Dittner had been able to identify Metz and another capo named Zimmermann as the main leaders in the infirmary. He had discovered that the hospital was being run as a separate unit from the rest of the camp. For some reason, an SS physician had independent control of the whole operation, and these two capos were allowed to do any sadistic thing they wished.

Once, Metz had been seen stomping a Pole in the doorway of the infirmary. Apparently, two other Poles had carried the man in only to be confronted with Metz's accusations that they were all trying to avoid work. After kicking the unconscious man in the groin, he had turned on the two friends with a leather belt. That night, the sick man died in his barracks.

No. 26 661 was struck by how ordinary Metz appeared. Standing at attention, he seemed to be just another prisoner. Yet he could apparently kill with ease.

With their dismissal, the work units assembled and once more No. 26 661 and the rest of the numbered throng began tramping through the snow. Metz turned toward the infirmary and his own "work."

Winter had not changed the nature of the tasks, and hauling dirt was only more painful in the cold. By 1 P.M., Christian was completely exhausted and felt numb all over. It was then that he spotted a man lying face down in the sludge of dirt and snow. Instantly, he realized that if an SS guard saw him, a club would begin to swing.

"Quickly!" he half-shouted to the nearest prisoner. "Help me pick him up." Reluctantly, the prisoner walked toward the slumped form.

Though he did not know him well, he recognized Heindrich Van Mohl as one of the Dutch prisoners. Because Van Mohl was completely unconscious, it made it all the more difficult to steady his weight between them. At least the guards couldn't argue that he was really capable of further work. In fact, as they struggled out of the field with his feet dragging in the snow, no one even paid much attention.

"Let's get him to the infirmary," No. 26 661 instructed the other prisoner.

"Look at his feet and hands," the man puffed.

"I'm sure the swelling means that edema has set in."

Trudging along, he thought about the night when Heindrich Van Mohl had first appeared in No. 26. The Dutch professor of theology had been caught hiding Jews in his house. In the overcrowded, smelly barracks, the tall, thin, and refined scholar, who appeared to have spent his life reading books, had become bewildered and disoriented. Obviously, the work of Dachau would soon devour him.

"I'm afraid his condition is very serious," the other prisoner speculated as they reached the door of the infirmary.

As the two men supported Van Mohl's weight between them, No. 26 661 knocked twice. A very well-fed Zimmermann opened it.

"This man is seriously ill," No. 26 661 said factually.

Zimmermann studied the situation for a moment, his eyes traveling across the red blotches on the Dutchman's neck and hands. His gaze shifted back and forth between the three men, narrowing as it went.

Then without a word, he swung his arm and smashed his fist into the center of Van Mohl's face. Before anyone could react, his other fist hit the right side of the professor's head. The force of the two blows sent all three men lurching backward.

"That's your medicine for today," the capo answered. "And if you two swine come back here again, I'll give each of you another treatment." Then he slammed the door in their faces.

"What will we do?" the prisoner cried. "We can't leave him here, but we'll be punished for taking him to the barracks."

"What else can we do?" No. 26 661 pondered. "He'll die in the fields today. We don't have much of a choice but to leave him inside regardless of what they do." Off they went down the bunker.

Once inside Barracks No. 26, they pushed Van Mohl as far back into the wooden beds as possible with the hope he'd be overlooked in a corner. Christian tried to stop the bleeding from Van Mohl's nose.

"Listen, I don't want anyone to know I've been a part of this," the helper warned. "I've fulfilled my responsibility and that's it."

"There are some things bigger than responsibility!" No. 26 661 snapped back.

"Look," the other prisoner leveled, "I know all about you pastors who are kept in here. And I'm no heathen. I was baptized on the earliest day my parents could bring me to the church. I respect what you're about. But I've done all I can."

"We all have a responsibility for each other," No. 26 661 charged. "That's just human."

"Ya," the man insisted, "and the Bible also says that living dogs are better than dead lions."

"Would you dare twist what Scripture says in a place like this?" Christian felt his anger becoming uncontrollable.

"All the same, leave me out of this."

"We are not animals unless we let them turn us into that," Reger shouted.

"Whatever you say, Pastor. All the same, I don't want anyone to know I was here."

"All right, all right!" he agreed as the prisoner quickly left the barracks.

Standing alone in the normally crowded barracks felt strange, yet wonderful. Perhaps, this one time they might overlook an obviously sick prisoner. Dittner had thought that the Cross should be a sword with which to strike enemies. *No,* Christian mused to himself, *it is a symbol of shared life, shared pain, of mutuality.*

"Well," he said to the unconscious man, "we did the best we could." With that, he shuffled back to the fields.

Three days later, with his face swollen and bruised, the Dutch theologian died.

Three

During the following days, the snow came down thick and heavy. In a night's time, one to two feet could accumulate. Soon, the prisoners recoiled at the sight of snowflakes in the air, for the SS had a strange compulsion about removing every vestige of the downfall from the camp. Moreover, the clergy were their favorite targets for work with the snow commando.

The commando of at least a thousand men would be rushed out into the streets to begin clearing them. Though the temperature was subfreezing and the shovels crude and makeshift, the group would be pushed at a furious pace for eight to ten hours.

"Tempo! Tempo! No delay!" crackled through the cold as teams of men scurried in every direction.

Wet, heavy snow would be carted off to the Würmbach River. If the carts were full, snow was piled on tables that required four men to lift and carry them. Eventually, men would become so exhausted that they would stumble and fall.

No. 26 661 worried about falling. Even in this brutal weather, sweat would pore out and soak his clothing. To fall or lie unconscious on the ground in that condition would make him a quick and easy target for pneumonia. Of course, being on the ground would further soak his clothing and there were *certainly* no dry ones to change into!

On this particular morning, a delay in getting the path open to the river allowed an unusual period of rest. Sitting next to him was a small, dark-complected man who leaned over to ask a question.

"You are a priest?" he inquired.

"No," No. 26 661 answered, rubbing his hands together to help the circulation. "I am a pastor of the Confessing Church."

"Oh, really!" the swarthy man said in a sort of delight. "I have known other men like you."

"You are a priest?" No. 26 661 asked the little man in return.

"Oh, no, no," he said rather cynically. "I am only a gypsy. That is why I am here. The Nazis don't like gypsies any better than they like Jews."

"I am sorry," the pastor said, not knowing what else to say.

"I came here from Buchenwald," the gypsy confided quietly. "I met a great man there who also was from your Confessing Church."

"Who?" No. 26 661 asked earnestly. The fate of any comrade was personal news.

"His name was Paul Schneider. He was the bravest man I've ever met," the gypsy said, as if divulging a sacred secret.

"Paul Schneider!" Christian exclaimed, gripping the man's arm. "Yes, I knew Paul Schneider! He was, indeed, a brother. What do you know of him?" He could feel the warmth of the gypsy's breath against his ear.

"The Nazis killed him!" he said bitterly. "Then they made me make a special flower wreath to put on the casket so it would appear to his widow that they had treated him honorably!" He stopped to spit disdainfully on the ground. "But I tell you, I never made anything with flowers so good in my life. Those pigs may have used my wreath to deceive his wife, but I made it to honor one of the best men God ever created."

Up ahead, the snow commando was starting to move again and the work was about to commence. They both stood up.

"I tell you, Pastor, sometimes I'm not sure what I believe," the gypsy said. "But I know this: whatever Paul Schneider stood for, I will believe in on the day I die."

"Move on!" the guards warned. "Stop wasting time!"

Whatever the obstacle to work had been, it was now removed. The convoy of wheelbarrows and huge wooden trays full of snow began to wind its exhausting way down to the river.

The gypsy had blended back into the stream of gray-striped uniforms and disappeared. From a short distance it was almost impossible to identify anyone, even a friend. There were so many things he wanted to ask the gypsy, but his attention was quickly directed back to the work.

The snow seemed even heavier than before. His mind fastened onto the gypsy's story. At first, he thought of what an extraordinary witness it was. Then, suddenly, nothing positive remained. All he could think of was that Paul Schneider was dead. They had killed him. They had killed Van Mohl. They had killed Werner Sylten. They had killed . . . they had killed . . . they had killed! The list didn't seem to end until he came to the thought, *And they will kill No. 26 661.* His mind hung there and couldn't seem to turn elsewhere. A vortex of despair sucked him down to its very center.

From out of the depths, other thoughts emerged. *What if I do fall? What if I do catch pneumonia? What if I do die? I no longer mean anything. I am nothing. I didn't even get the name of the gypsy. So what. What's the difference? What if I had given him my name? None of this means anything. Nothing is left. Nothing will remain.*

Though the sunlight seemed to dazzle with new brilliance as it bounced off the snow, inside, the deepest darkness was settling over all hope. *The Nazis have made us to be as worthless as dung,* he accused himself. *Why should I even keep trying to go on? In the end, they will win. They have won!*

As he bent over his shovel, staring at the ground and ready to quit, another idea ventured into his imagination as if by its own force. From somewhere long ago, from some forgotten catechism class, a simple sentence reappeared: "I have called thee by thy name." It echoed again and again. "I have called *thee* by thy name. I have called thee *by* thy name. I have called thee by thy *name*."

As he searched his memory for the time when he had memorized that verse, other memories surfaced too. He remembered his extraordinary seminary experience, when Christ had come to him in a blinding flash of light. When he had been unsure of his faith, that moment had confirmed that Christ was and would be with him. The warmth of that light once more pervaded his doubts.

Then the red and green matchbox that had been slipped to him in Schneidemühl prison danced before his eyes. Just thinking about it was like a surge of hope.

When he hadn't been sure of his faith, confirmation had come. The matchbox had taught him how God is present even in the smallest of things. No! He was not just a number! He had a name and God still called him by his name.

"I may be poor, isolated, and beaten down," he thought aloud, "but I will never be annihilated!"

Another Scripture came to mind. "We are saved by this hope."

"No! The Nazis have not won!" he found himself muttering under his breath. "Glory to God, I do have a name! I am not forgotten! I will thank Him that in this moment there is sunlight!"

Overhearing some of these words, a prisoner next to him looked up with a startled expression at what he thought he had heard. Christian nodded his head and shook his fist in defiance at all that was around him. The prisoner was perplexed.

"And you are not nameless either!" Christian said suddenly as he passed him, wheeling his cart toward the river. "You are called by a name—have hope!"

CHAPTER FIVE △
A LIGHT IN THE DARKNESS—1942

One

"YOU WILL NOT BELIEVE what I heard!" Dittner whispered in Christian's ear as they leaned against the barracks wall. The intense cold caused each of them to tightly cross their arms as if to force all possible body heat back inside their skins.

"What?" Christian answered shortly, trying not to waste even the warmth of his breath.

"Our hidden radios picked up an astonishing report. Sometime in December the Americans entered the war on the side of the British."

"Really?" Christian's hands dropped to his sides. "The United States is in the war!"

"Ya, that's the news."

"What does this mean?"

"No one seems to know, but it is clear that the Nazi propaganda has changed its direction somewhat. The new party line is that we must now defend our victories."

"Maybe that's why our food has become so meager." Christian realized again how constant was his own gnawing hunger.

"I tell you," Dittner said, gripping Reger's arm, "God is not ignoring what has happened in Germany! His judgment has already been announced by those radios."

Karl Leisner and Leonard Steinwender overheard him and immediately turned to join the discussion.

"You believe judgment is coming on us?" Leonard probed.

"Like a beast being shot down in the entrance to its lair!" growled Dittner. "God hasten the day!" With that he moved on to share the news with other men.

"How hard it is," said Karl, "to love your country and hate its government."

A train whistle from somewhere beyond the barbed-wire fence interrupted the conversation. The sound signaled the arrival of another load of human cargo and reminded them that the endless flow never quite seemed to satisfy the insatiable appetite of Dachau.

"How can they pack any more men in here?" Leonard wondered aloud, and shook his head. "Space is gone and the food rations are becoming critical."

"All-consuming hate runs this place," Karl declared and his eyes blazed with emotion. "Nothing rational can explain it!"

"Nazi fanaticism is like a disease that infects your feelings and then moves on to eat at your mind, until finally it devours your heart and soul."

"Fanaticism is like that, Leonard," Christian mused. "It takes a part of life and makes it the whole. The fanatic believes his cause to be the center of the world."

"And any of his actions are justified in the name of that cause," Karl said, pushing his glasses back up the bridge of his nose. "I think a conscious dishonesty is involved. Look at the great lengths that Goebels must go to deceive the nation."

"You know," Reger added, "it is possible even for Christians to become such fanatics. Even our zeal can become twisted."

"And is not dying for the cause a strangely seductive invitation?" Leonard asked.

"Certainly!" Karl answered. "Every one of us wants to be absolutely right. And martyrdom seems to allow us the chance to baptize our yearning and seal it with an eternal promise."

"So," Christian pondered, "how do we not shrink back and still not be seduced?"

"We must never forget what it means to be sinful men." Karl slowly and carefully chose his words. The deacon's natural humility forged his insights with their own mettle of truth. "Only God's mercy overrules our misinterpretations and blunders. We all can be so quickly victimized when our pride is disguised as light."

"I think that is why real courage transcends itself," Leonard offered, sitting down on the bed. "While the fanatic is zealous because he is convinced he is absolutely right, true courage never has such certainty. All we can do is try our best to get beyond ourselves."

"The cross," said Karl, reaching for his crucifix before remembering it had been stripped away by the guards, "the cross is truly a symbol of courage as well as of sacrificial love. In this place, it is the only true power we will ever have, but I must believe that in the end it will have been enough."

"The chapel is prepared for worship," someone shouted from the doorway that led into the front room. Immediately, the trio stopped talking and turned to crowd into the place that had become the true center of warmth for No. 26. Each man found it hard to move forward as the "bedroom" had swollen to almost 200 men in a space about 70 feet square.

Inside, several of the Catholic clerics had moved two tables together to form an altar and had covered the rough wood with a white sheet. From somewhere, two candles and a figure of Christ had appeared. In the center, an empty tin can had been cut and shaped into a shining monstrance. An Austrian Communist had secretly made the little worship symbol and smuggled it into the barracks as a token of admiration for the pastors' courage. Only one mass a month was allowed and only one priest could be the celebrant.

As Christian entered the chapel, a Polish priest suddenly but weakly grabbed his arm with an emaciated hand. The man slumped against the door jamb and began to slide down. "I can't go on, and I am the celebrant tonight," he groaned. His coarse hair fell down into his eyes as his head rested against the wall.

"Here, let me help you," Christian said, and tried to support him.

"I'm starving," the priest confessed. "I think I'm going to faint."

"I can help you stand." Christian gripped his arm. "Don't give up. You will be able to celebrate the mass tonight if I have to hold you up."

"I'm afraid I just can't continue," he sighed deeply. "I must eat first or I know I will collapse at the altar."

The prisoners surrounding them spread the word through the barracks.

From somewhere a hidden crust of bread miraculously appeared. Quickly it was passed to the priest. He savored each minute bite as if it might multiply within him. Whether it was the thought of the food or the charity of the gift which energized him, within minutes he was ready to go on with the service. Relief rippled through the group.

Catholics, Protestants, Orthodox all knelt together. The many backgrounds blended together as surely as the uniforms and haircuts removed all visible marks of rank or distinction.

Christian watched the men around him drop to their knees. *What an amazing transformation!* he thought to himself. *Clergy who have warred with each other for centuries are praying as brothers. No longer does anyone argue over dogmas or differing opinions.*

"Only one thing matters," the Polish priest began. "Jesus Christ is among us tonight."

As Christian dropped to his knees, he felt the deepest personal confirmation.

The priest's prayer lacked polished oratory and yet it communicated with a reality of conviction that lifted each man's heart and with it his sense of dignity.

"Thou art joy in all our sorrow," was started by a song leader in the midst of the group. The chorus of men poured out, "O Thou loving Jesus Christ, source Thou art of all of heaven's bounty, true and only Saviour Christ!"

"No amount of starvation," Christian whispered to the man next to him, "can keep us from the nourishment of these words."

"Let us hear God's words." The priest opened a little Bible that had made its way past the SS in the Jourhaus. "In your weakness is My strength made perfect," he read slowly and loudly.

"In this a-a-a difficult place, one can learn fully what such words mean." The priest began his exposition haltingly. His German was not good and he struggled to be clear. "Also, God giving now to us special opportunity in such place to experience His promises." He gripped the table with his bony hands to steady himself.

"You must see Jesus Christ is perfect combination of power and goodness. But when He came among us, He was here in complete powerlessness. He refused to use power."

Christian thought of Dittner and wondered what he might think about this frail man whose words rang with force.

"Is cross a symbol of power? Not to the ancient Romans!" The priest struck the altar feebly. "But in the end it conquered them with most irresistible power in the world—the might of irresistible love! Such love that is willing to suffer for the redemption of others contains overwhelming power of goodness able to truly conquer even ultimate evil!"

As the priest turned to complete the mass, his words burned in Christian's mind. Warmth had begun to rise up at the center of his being and a wave of peace swept over him. He felt comforted, consoled, reassured. Things that could not be explained or reconciled seemed to no longer matter. He prepared to receive the sacrament. When the words of the last hymn died away, the men slowly drifted out of the chapel. Little was said until they were back in the larger room.

"The priest's words touched me tonight," Christian told Leonard.

"Not me!" Dittner answered from the wooden bed. "I don't understand such talk about powerlessness overcoming the world. It is contradiction; it is nonsense."

"No, you wouldn't," Leonard replied, shaking his head without seeming condescending. "It's a paradox. Catholics have always known about this secret of the crucifix. It is the mystery of how God is with us when everything else in the world seems to deny His existence."

Dittner only shook his head.

"I once had an amazing experience of God's presence," Christian said, turning to Leonard, "at a time when I felt totally lost during my second year in seminary."

Suddenly the overhead lights went out and the room was plunged into darkness. As in some children's game where the loser becomes "it," men frantically scurried for places on the wooden racks. Christian and Leonard quickly slid in beside Dittner.

"Well?" Dittner asked in the darkness. "What happened to you?"

"I was very confused because my faith had no certainty," Christian began. "I had never experienced any personal confirmation of what I professed to be true. Really, I doubted the very faith I was preparing to proclaim."

"Please, a little louder," some prisoner down the line requested.

"Strange as it may sound, I was studying one of Plato's essays about the problem of knowing anything with certainty. He wrote that everyone needs some anchor to hold him steady in the pursuit of reality." Christian tried to lie flat, but it was difficult being wedged between two men so tightly.

"Ya! Ya!" another voice confirmed. "I believe that too."

"I was in such despair that I began to pray fervently that God would give me such an anchor. I was truly heartbroken when I finally pleaded, 'Lord Jesus, please be real to me. Please come into my life and live again in what I am and what I do.'"

"What happened?" asked Leonard.

"Ya, what happened?" someone on the left implored.

"Please." Christian felt very uncomfortable not knowing who was listening. "I am very hesitant about sharing this story. I know that it is unusual and, well, I don't want anyone to get a wrong impression of me."

"Of course," another nameless voice answered him. "We are all sensitive to these matters. Just tell us your experience."

"Well," he said, propping himself up on his elbow, "it was like a magnificent explosion of light bursting upon my tiny room. Like a Roman candle on a summer night. Each part of my room was bathed in the warmth of a wondrous, healing radiance. Without any comprehension, I tumbled from my bed to my knees. My meager bedroom had become holy ground."

"What was the light like?" quizzed Dittner.

"It was not a kindly light as much as a terrible flash of brilliance. I buried my face in my hands and tried to say something, but 'O my Lord!' was all I could repeat. And then the light was gone. As quickly as the radiance had come, it ceased. Then a passage of Scripture began to run through my mind: 'For the same God who said, "Light shall shine out of darkness," has shined in our hearts, to give the light of the knowledge of the glory of God in the face of Jesus Christ.' "

"Do you believe this really happened?" Dittner's voice was more hopeful than skeptic.

"At times I wondered whether it was all in my head. Yet afterward, I knew that *I* was different."

"Rationalists like me have no fondness for visions and mysteries," Dittner confessed. "Yet I don't doubt you."

"So the night is never as dark as it seems," Leonard concluded, "or as long as we might wish. Thank you for trusting us with such an experience."

Two

"No. 26 661?" the SS guard screamed.

The sky was still black; it felt more like night than morning. Christian ducked his head and tried to appear inconspicuous. The only way to avoid extra abuse was to be unseen.

"Where are you, 26 661?" the guard demanded.

"They're after you for helping the Dutch theologian," Dittner whispered.

"I was afraid they'd get you sooner or later for bringing Van Mohl back here," Leonard said, stepping in front of Reger to further shield him from view.

"You worthless pig! Step this way or I will strangle you with your own towel." The guard pushed his way through the men in the barracks. "Here is a lesson for every one of you to learn!"

Timidly, Christian stepped out from behind his cover of fellow prisoners.

"Look at this towel!" the guard yelled to the whole barracks. "It is dry! No. 26 661 has not washed himself."

Silence fell over the whole group. Obviously, no towels had been used that early in the morning. Most of the time, the crowding was so bad no one ever saw a towel anyway.

"Are we going to tolerate such filth and unconcern? Are you going to allow your fellow prisoner to contaminate your clean barracks that the Reich has so graciously provided?"

No one made a sound, but all understood the real message.

"No. 26 661, you are to serve as an example to this group! We will teach you a little lesson about taking care of things." Grabbing the back of Reger's striped shirt, the guard jerked him toward the door. "Since you do not appreciate the services we have provided, some time by yourself will sharpen your manners."

Pushed out the front door of the barracks, Christian found himself standing with a "select group" of prisoners from other barracks. Apparently, the guards had staged an early morning roundup for a number of men marked for special punishment.

"*Snell! Snell!*" The guards double-timed the group down the bunker.

"O God!" a prisoner next to him moaned. "I hope they don't put me up on the stake."

Christian was able to glance down at the emblem on the man's shirt and see that he too was a political prisoner. Obviously, his thin arms wouldn't take much strain. If they did put him on the stake, he could be hung for hours with his wrists chained behind his back and pulled up high enough that his heels could no longer touch the ground.

"Shut up, fools, or it will be worse!" crackled over their heads as they marched down to the detention cells.

"No. 26 661, here's a place for you to think about our rules," the guard said indifferently as he pushed him into a small room that couldn't have been any more than 30 inches square.

"This is a great place for you to see the light," he chuckled as he slammed the door, leaving Reger in total darkness. "A couple days' rest in here will be good for you."

So, Christian thought to himself, *this is the 'standing bunker' where you have to stand day and night. Surely, this can't be too bad.*

However, the creeping movement of time soon revealed the diabolical nature of the cage. Though he might try to slump against the sides to rest, there was no way for his body to get any real relief or relaxation. His muscles began to ache and finally to cramp. His only light was that which came in when the bread and water meal was pushed through the door.

Sometime later in the day, or perhaps night, or maybe it was the next morning, or maybe the next week, his imagination began to play strange tricks. No longer could he tell whether it was morning or evening. Time seemed scrambled together in a jumbled, hazy twilight that was neither sleep nor alertness. He thought only about eating, and imagined food as an adolescent boy dreams of women. Hunger and heaviness hung over his mind like a veil.

Once, in the strange flow of timelessness, he heard a voice coming from another cell. As he listened intently, he knew he had heard the voice before; perhaps it was an old friend. Could he be hallucinating?

Then he realized whose voice it was. Niemöller! The man in the next cell was Martin Niemöller! Although he had looked for Niemöller for days, he had never seen him in the camp.

Immediately, Christian thought he would call to Niemöller, but then realized there was no way to know who might be listening on either side. If he called out, it might endanger everyone. So he just pressed his ear even more closely against the wall to hear anything he could.

A few more words came through and then everything faded away; but his mind had become crystal clear! The spell of solitary confinement was broken! The tortuous scheme had been defeated because he was reminded that he really wasn't alone.

And once again he remembered the matchbox and how it had first taught him that truth. "That is the key to everything," he decided "I must remember that I am not alone"

The darkness of his cubicle didn't really seem that different from the much larger cell at Schneidemühl prison. His mind's eye began to recreate those final days before he was shipped to Dachau. The loneliness and solitude of being cut off from his wife and of not having any idea of what was ahead had eaten away the veneer of his self-confidence. Depression, like a shroud, had closed around him worse than any he had ever experienced. God seemed to have disappeared and he had lost all touch with the things that he believed.

No longer had he cared what he looked like. He quit washing his face and combing his hair, and sat in the corner of the cell staring at the wall. Time started to slip past him and he lost track of the days and weeks. Then in the midst of his utter hopelessness, a letter had been tossed through the cell-door window.

Of course, it had already been opened and read by the secret police. The postmark read June 11, 1940. Three weeks had passed since Mina had been to see him. Slowly, he realized how badly he had lost his grip on reality.

Yet he knew immediately that the letter was from Mina, and that recognition was like a knife cutting through his mental fog. Eagerly, hungrily, he fumbled at the envelope to get the pages out.

She was all right. Her health was good. Nothing harmful had happened to her, to their house, or to the church. Life was going routinely and the congregation was concerned for him and praying for his well-being. Just reading those words began to make Christian feel alive again.

To encourage him, Mina had written out Acts 4:26-30:

> Why did the Gentiles rage, and the peoples imagine vain things? The kings of the earth set themselves in array, and the rulers were gathered together, against the Lord, and against His Anointed.

For of a truth in this city against Thy holy servant Jesus, whom Thou didst anoint, both Herod and Pontius Pilate, with the Gentiles and the peoples of Israel, were gathered together, to do whatsoever Thy hand and Thy counsel foreordained to come to pass. And now, Lord, look upon their threatenings: and grant unto Thy servants to speak Thy Word with all boldness, while Thou stretchest forth Thy hand to heal; and that signs and wonders may be done through the name of Thy holy servant Jesus.

Christian could only sit there wondering why Mina had sent this particular passage. He felt as if he would never again have confidence, much less boldness.

Before he could finish the rest of the letter, the door of his cell had swung open and a guard had beckoned him to follow.

"Do I need my things?" he asked, fearing this might be his final exit.

"No, leave them. You are going only for a judicial inquiry."

"What does that mean?"

"Follow me!" The guard was harsh and unconcerned.

As they walked down the narrow corridor, Christian could see a fellow prisoner, a clergyman, coming toward them. Even though he did not know the cleric well, he had heard of his arrest. The man had dared to hold a worship service on Ascension Day, the day Hitler was preparing to attack Russia. Hitler had forbidden any services on that holy day because they might affect the people's view of the war.

The approaching prisoner kept looking into Christian's eyes as if he were trying to tell him something. As Christian and his guard turned sideways to let him and his guard pass, the man thrust a small matchbox into Christian's hand. Quickly, Christian slipped it into his pocket as they passed.

Though Christian wondered what was in the matchbox, his mind was on the inquiry. Often Jewish and Polish prisoners were tortured during these "inquiries." However, to his relief, the interrogation was brief, without violence, and he was quickly on his way back to the cell with the final words of the Gestapo officer ringing in his head. "You are to leave immediately for Dachau Concentration Camp. *Seig Heil!*"

Entering the cell, he began gathering his things until he knew the guard was gone and the peephole was closed. Then he sat down to look inside the matchbox.

The contents were nothing but a small piece of paper. He unfolded it and found written, "Read Acts 4:26-30."

Acts 4:26-30? Quickly, he rummaged through the pile on his bunk searching for Mina's letter. He pulled it open to check, and there it was! Mina had quoted the exact same passage, Acts 4:26-30!

Two people with no possible contact had sent him exactly the same message within 10 minutes. Only God could arrange such a thing! He had intervened to show Christian that he remained under His special care. He wasn't abandoned! He wasn't alone! The care of the Heavenly Father had reached through all of the Gestapo's security and surveillance.

He again looked at the bottom lines of Mina's letter: "And now, Lord, look upon their threatenings: and grant unto Thy servants to speak Thy Word with all boldness, while Thou stretchest forth Thy hand to heal; and that signs and wonders may be done through the name of Thy holy servant Jesus."

A wave of joy and relief swept over him, and with it the icy grip of despair melted away. What had been lost in that cell was found again. Before, he had not been able to remember a single word of consolation, but now they seemed to pour in upon him.

"Peace I leave with you; My peace I give unto you: not as the world giveth, give I unto you." He recalled what Martin Luther had written about that passage. The world assumes that peace comes only when a burden is taken away. If a man is poor, he thinks of becoming rich If a dying man can escape death, he believes he will have peace. But Luther taught this is not how Christ gives peace. On the contrary, Christ often allows the burden to lay on us. Rather than taking the burden from the person, he takes the person from the burden!

Christian had been left to struggle with his burden during the weeks of solitary confinement in order to discover the most important lesson he could learn. Pain and difficulties remained, but now he knew the source of a new strength which would allow him to stand under the load and to speak "with all boldness."

Placing his face in his hands, he wept. The dread he had felt at coming to the end of his confinement was strangely gone. The days ahead at Dachau would be much harder, yet he could endure.

A splinter gouged his leg, reminding him of where he was. In his standing cell, all of those memories had taken on a necessary immediacy. Over and over, he recalled the lines of Scripture Mina had sent. Shifting his weight, he once more tried to rest against the wall and this time drifted off to sleep.

Three

"How was your vacation?" August Schmidt asked with the usual twinkle in his eye.

"Most relaxing and restful," Christian answered, looking straight ahead. You could get away with talking during assembly roll calls if you didn't look as though you were carrying on a conversation. "I found Niemöller."

"Really! They did accommodate you well."

"He was in the cell just on the other side of the wall."

"Good! How are you feeling?"

"Starved!"

"We are all hungry." As he spoke, it was obvious he had lost another tooth. "The food rations are even fewer than before."

"*Auchtung!*" blasted over the loudspeaker and the men sprang to attention. "To your assignments!" Since the snow had begun to melt and the arctic cold was gone, work seemed more bearable. What's more, Christian had been given additional responsibility—he was now one of the cooks.

But as the spring wore on, he slowly began to realize that a subtle and deadly game was being played with the food. On visiting days or times of special review, the menu was made to look adequate. The next day, rations were cut back to compensate for any extra food consumed the preceding day. On regular working days, the food was never adequate. In fact, the soup became increasingly diluted.

At the same time, the radios told them of the great victories Germany was amassing. Each broadcast made it sound as if every German was now living in abundance. Nevertheless, the prisoners were becoming weaker and weaker.

When Reger carried buckets of food into the fields, he could sense that hunger was beginning to rule. Men were desperate and anxious at the sight of food. They would crowd and push to get near. However, once the bowl was filled with watery soup and a man had received his single piece of bread, cruel disappointment remained in his eyes.

Conversations seemed inevitably to turn to food. "How can they feed us so poorly if the war is going so well?" a prisoner would ask. "Do you think there will be more vegetables in the soup today?" another would continue. "I remember the bread my wife used to bake," a third would add.

Even Christian's reflections about Mina competed with the intrusive thoughts of hunger. She had always been the dearest desire of his heart, but he found he didn't think about her as often as before. He was becoming obsessed with food.

With the coming of summer, work began at 4 in the morning.

The early hour and the summer sun caused a drain on energy and strength that was not being replenished. Though the flow of new prisoners was endless, nothing could mask the mounting daily count of dead bodies. They were dying from sheer exhaustion and deprivation.

One of the prisoners coined the phrase, "the death summer." Quickly, it spread throughout the camp. "We are in the death summer of '42," men confided to each other.

By the end of July, the buckets of food had become almost more than Christian could carry. He dreaded the times he had to trudge out into the fields with those heavy weights hanging from his shoulders. Yet at 5 in the morning, noon, and 7 at night he staggered into the fields.

Starvation was taking its toll in every direction. Even August Schmidt had to be taken to the infirmary. Many of the prisoners were losing control of their emotions.

One evening as Christian entered the barracks, he immediately noticed that one of the sleeping racks was shaking. A prisoner name Husar was rolled up in a ball and crying uncontrollably, his arms pulled up over his face.

"What is it, Husar?" Christian said, shaking him.

He didn't respond, but only seemed to curl up more tightly.

Christian pleaded, "Let me help you!" There was no reply. He knew Husar lacked nothing in courage. Because this pastor had publicly protested the Nazis' program of euthanasia, he had been sent to Dachau. Surely, only the bravest of men would accuse the Nazis in public!

Slowly, Husar began to recognize Christian. "I can't stand it any longer!" he sobbed. "I can't bear any more!"

"Yes, you can," Christian assured him. "You must! You must keep on."

Christian prayed frantically—words of encouragement, hope, and comfort. Finally, he gently rocked the man to sleep.

Christian thought to himself, *How hard it is to live what we believe.*

At times, the answers seem to trickle through our fingers and we can't grasp the very things we thought were most important. None of us are heroes. We just do the best we can, and try to survive. Perhaps tomorrow night Husar will comfort me when I try to sleep.

Yet the next day's rounds came without relief. At noon, Christian sat down in the field to eat with the rest of the prisoners. Glancing at the ground, he noticed some rather tender-looking plants growing at his feet. Since they were cultivating such plants, he reasoned that surely they would be edible. So he put several stems into his soup.

Within minutes, he knew something was extremely wrong. Stomach cramps began to double him over.

"I'm sick, I'm sick!" he moaned, rolling in agony.

Looking into his bowl, a prisoner quickly saw why. "For God's sake, man! You've eaten some of the digitalis plants we're cultivating. That stuff will murder you!"

"Help! Help!" Christian called out as he staggered to his feet and down the rows. "My stomach is killing me." But no one reached out as he reeled down the road to the infirmary.

His obvious pain and weakness kept the nurses from rejecting him. Even Capo Metz gave him a quick look and nodded for the nurses to put him to bed. Cramps made his abdomen feel like one gigantic knot. His whole body pulsated with the effects of the poison. Finally, he slipped into a swirling, fitful sleep. Once more, time lost meaning and existing was all that was left.

Several days later, Christian was able to get out of bed and walk very slowly to the bathroom for the first time. On one of these trips, he saw a set of scales in the corner. Checking his weight seemed like a good exercise.

"Oh no!" he gasped. "These weights must be wrong."

To his left, a male nurse was scrubbing the floor. He looked up and solemnly affirmed, "They are right."

"No," Reger insisted. "When I entered this place, I weighed 198 pounds. These scales can't be correct."

"What do they say?" the nurse asked.

"Ninety-five pounds!"

"Look at yourself," the nurse said in disgust. "Look what they have done to you. Just look at your legs."

"I've lost a hundred pounds!"

The male nurse cast an eye around the room to see who was listening. "You better get yourself out of here or you'll lose the rest of it," he warned.

Christian leaned against the infirmary wall. "I had no idea I was this bad," he admitted.

The nurse went back to his scrubbing and Christian tried to order his thoughts. He found himself going completely blank.

"August?" He suddenly remembered August Schmidt was here somewhere.

"Do you know where a prisoner named Schmidt might be?" he asked the nurse. "August Schmidt is his name."

The nurse didn't raise his head, but continued as if he hadn't heard him.

Christian limped a little closer to the capo. "August is a friend of mine. He came here maybe two weeks ago."

The nurse shook his head and kept scrubbing.

"Who could I ask about him?" he persisted.

"Don't!" the capo said abruptly. "Mind your own business and you'll live longer."

"Please," Christian said, tugging at the capo's shirt. "Please tell me what you know. This man is a good friend."

Once again looking around the room, the nurse dropped the brush into the bucket. "He's gone. The whole batch of them is gone."

"He went back to the barracks?"

"No, you fool! Don't you understand? The SS cleaned house in here and put all of them on the transports just before you came in. By now they have gassed him. Now don't ask me any more of your idiotic questions."

August's impish, toothless smile and cheerful face were all that Christian could see. The priest had always been able to find some humorous twist even in the worst moments. And now he was gone. So many had "disappeared" that Christian could no longer feel the loss and pain that he had in the beginning. Yet the little priest had been very important to him. However, the grief that might have welled up within him was pushed aside by the realization that if August had been taken, he could go too.

"I've got to get out of here." Christian grabbed the end of a bed as desperation seized him. "He's right. I've got to get out of here." But all he remembered later was falling on a bed before he lost consciousness.

Not until the next morning did he awake. The capo who cared for that section of the infirmary was shaking men and warning them not to go into the washroom.

"Wait a while before you go to the bathroom," he told Reger.

"Why?" Christian's body ached so bad that he was in no hurry to get up.

"Dead men are in there. They died during the night and their bodies haven't been moved yet. Wait 30 minutes or so and we will have removed them."

Only then did Christian fully realize that August Schmidt was dead. The evening's conversation came back in bits and pieces that slowly blended into the horror that was all around him. His mind and emotions were so severely assaulted that he couldn't really respond to his friend's death. The only thought that made any difference was getting out of there. *The transports are going to come for another load any time now,* he worried.

Reaching for a strength that he didn't know was there, he walked from the bed to Capo Metz's desk.

"I am ready to return to work," he mumbled.

"Then get out!" Metz's full face was an obvious reminder of where the food went. "Your name will go off our roll right now."

"Oh, thank you, thank you." Christian felt ingratiating, but nevertheless he was alive.

He wasn't sure *how* he was alive or, at that moment, *why* he was alive. As he limped back to the fields still holding his shrunken stomach, he was only aware of the very singular fact that once more he had survived. Living didn't feel very good, but he thought it must in some way be a gift.

CHAPTER SIX   △

PREY FOR
THE BEAST—1942

One

"THINGS ARE CHANGING," Dittner puffed, as the group trotted down the bunker.

"Ah, but the autumn weather is such a relief from the death summer!" Christian panted.

"Not just the weather—look around you."

Christian took a quick glance at the barracks and the streets that led off the bunker. Everywhere, men were milling around or working tightly together. Surprisingly, many of them were wearing civilian clothes, not striped prison uniforms.

"A lot of people died last summer," Dittner explained, and nodded in the direction of the infirmary. "But for everyone who died, two more came in. Things are not going so good with the war."

"Company halt!" The SS guard stopped the convoy of men. In the center of the assembly ground, a large pile of clothing in all shapes and sizes was strewn on the ground. The prisoners could even see some women's and children's garments intermingled with the rest. The guard walked here and there among the items picking up a few pieces that caught his attention. Satisfied, he ordered, "All right, get what you want."

The prisoners leaped into the pile of clothing, grabbing and snatching anything that looked warm and durable. Even though the memory of summer heat hung in their minds, every man knew how quickly that would change.

"Where'd all this stuff come from?" a new prisoner with the criminal's patch on his shirt asked.

"Where do you think?" Christian answered sarcastically.

"Auschwitz—Buchenwald—the castle at Linz," Dittner snapped.

"Humph!" the man grunted without comprehension.

Smiles broke out everywhere as the men recognized the vast improvement in their appearance. Some of the clothing was of remarkably good quality and condition. But as the men explored their new garments, the mood slowly changed.

"What a wool coat!" exclaimed Christian, tucking his hands in the pockets and feeling the thickness of the material. At the bottom his fingers found something.

"Look at this!" Dittner pulled out ticket stubs to a theater in Prague.

In turn, Christian produced an old tram ticket from a train in Budapest.

Other men began to hold up pictures of children or letters that had been hastily scribbled on the backs of envelopes. Knowing glances were exchanged, but nothing more was said. They picked what they knew they needed and got back in line.

"My, my," Dittner remarked as he folded the coat over his arm. "What a clever way to economize on prison uniforms."

"Move on," the guard demanded. "Others need their turn here. Get on to the mess hall."

"Things *are* changing," Dittner insisted as they stepped into line "Notice the food today."

Christian extended his wooden bowl to receive his meal. Having worked in the food lines, he had a keen eye about the quality. "There seems to be a little more here."

"Ya," Dittner smiled. "Slowly but surely, they have been adding a little more to the soup."

"I'm not getting fat. What do you make of it?"

"Well, they're not giving us much more, but there is increased nourishment. It all confirms my suspicions." Dittner sat down on the ground with his bowl carefully balanced so that not a drop would be lost.

"So?"

"They've given me a new job." He pointed with his thumb toward a long factory building far beyond the other side of the fence. "I'm to work on electric cables for Messerschmitt engines. This isn't any of that dirt-moving nonsense. I'm going to be doing serious production."

"So?"

"Ever since we've been here, they've obviously been trying to kill us. Now, they're changing their direction. They really want us to produce. In fact," and with this he leaned over to whisper, "I've discovered that the SS is even going to allow us to receive food parcels."

"Really!" Christian scraped the bottom of his bowl an extra time.

"Now, here's the clincher. The radios tell us the army attacked Stalingrad and lost. Even the propaganda line isn't able to explain the trouble on the Russian front. As best we can tell, the Allies have either taken Italy or are about to."

"Are you sure of all of this?"

"Absolutely!" Dittner glanced around once more. "It adds up. At first, we were garbage to them; now, the able-bodied are needed for production. So, they will feed us better."

Christian watched the smoke drift across the camp toward the river. "All this may be good news and then again it may not."

"Why?" Dittner grunted.

"They may fatten us up a bit, but if the war goes badly, we may be the first to go."

"Aha!" Dittner laughed cynically and slapped him on the back. "You have learned to think like a prisoner—a survivor. I'm proud of you. Dachau has taught you a little something."

Reger stood up and said nothing.

"Mark my words," Dittner predicted as they walked along, "they'll be finding you a new job. Political prisoners have more value to them than do the convicts and the Jews."

As they started across the assembly ground, a group of prisoners crossed in front of them pushing wooden carts covered with heavy cloth. Here and there a leg or arm was sticking out.

Grabbing the arm of one of the cartpushers, Dittner demanded, "What is this all about?"

"A transport train just came in from Duisburg. They didn't make it."

Refusing to let go of his sleeve, Dittner persisted. "Look at the size of this load! What happened?"

The prisoner leaned toward him and said quickly, "They were locked in for weeks without food. Some parts of these bodies have been gnawed right down to the bone!"

Immobilized, Dittner dropped the sleeve and the subject. The prisoner hurried to catch up with the cart as it turned toward the crematoriums. Christian felt his whole body become rigid and his stomach flinch.

"Some things have not changed much," he said.

Two

"No. 26 661 reporting for new assignment, Sir."

Drawing himself to his full six feet, the young man standing in front of Christian was almost visibly flexing his muscles. Surely, he couldn't be much more than 22 or 23, for there was yet a soft boyishness about his face. He adjusted his belt and coat buttons in a calculated manner.

"I am Lieutenant Herman Boye and I will not tolerate any inefficiency." He walked slowly around his new assignee as if he were a general inspecting a private. Obviously, he was Aryan down to his toenails, the blond-haired, blue-eyed sort of youth that Hitler idealized.

"You are an enemy of the government, the people, our Führer. In former times, people like you didn't live long. Indeed, you should consider yourself fortunate that you were not shot after your arrest."

He stopped abruptly and stared at the prisoner as if expecting confirmation. No. 26 661 nodded slightly.

"But you are even less," Boye snorted contemptuously. "You are one of the narrowminded preachers who make people stupid. You are a teacher of nonsense." After a pause, he asked, "Don't you have anything to say?" His thin lips were tight and smirking. With his feet at parade rest, he turned sideways so that he wouldn't even have to look at Christian.

"I'm, ah, not sure what you mean, is all." No. 26 661 tried to sound apologetic even though his very response implied a challenge.

The lieutenant seemed delighted to have further opportunity to lecture. "Take the so-called Sermon on the Mount with its teaching of turning the other cheek." When he turned back and pointed at Christian, it was obvious that his white, manicured hands had never seen physical labor. "Between you and the Jews, the whole nation has suffered the humiliation of being made poor at the hands of our enemies! Now National Socialism has risen up with power and might to crush any who oppose or hinder us!"

Through the office window, No 26 661 could see about 15

Jewish-looking prisoners harnessed together behind wooden poles and chains pulling huge rollers down the street. The first snow had already started to accumulate. Normally, it would take at least two strong horses to pull such rollers. As the exhausted men strained forward, the SS guards and capos yelled and cracked leather whips above the prisoners' heads.

"I will not tolerate any sloth or distractions in this office!"

Reger's mind snapped back. He realized he had lost the drift of the lecture and wasn't sure what his response should be.

"You will be a clerk here and I expect you to expend the same energy you would have in the fields. This office is no vacation."

Christian surveyed the door and the windows. No snow was blowing in here and there were stoves at both ends of the room.

"All of the salaries are prepared in these offices, so your work is of some value. You should be grateful to us."

His mind started to wander again. He felt rather guilty in thanking God for not being on the rollers or out in the fields as were other men. On the other hand, just being in such a warm room might make all the difference in surviving another winter. He had developed a habit of praying about such things, but he wasn't sure what was right under these circumstances.

"When you come to appreciate what National Socialism has brought to our Fatherland, you may be of service to your country again." The boy officer stood with his arms crossed, his starched, straight stance and leather riding boots making him look like the master of all destiny. "Your attitude in this office will be carefully observed and your repentance noted."

Once more, No. 26 661 humbly nodded. This was indeed an odd scenario—as if he were a child caught in sin being sent for penance to an unrelenting priest. Christian knew he must not provoke any confrontations.

"You are seeing a rare lesson in courage these days," Boye continued. "On all sides are men who will gladly die for their convictions. Observe us Nazis well for we can teach you about the power of faith."

No. 26 661 stared straight ahead without emotion.

"All of my life I have watched men like you, men like my father. You were weaned on worry; worry about money, worry about the French, worry about the British, worry about the Communists. I grew up surrounded by doubt and fear. He used to rub his rosary beads like they were Aladdin's lamp, but nothing ever happened."

Christian shifted his weight.

"But when Hitler came, the worry and the want stopped! Der Führer has given my generation hope. I am not like my father because I know the future. It belongs to us. It belongs to me!"

Leaning into Christian's face, his blue eyes narrowed. "You can't understand that, can you?

"Well, Mr. Preacher, you will come to see that we are right because we are superior. Because we believe in ourselves, we will prevail. We are truly invincible."

Clearly pleased with this beginning, the lieutenant swaggered back to his desk. "Someone will be here shortly to tell you what to do. Sit down and be quiet until we call for you."

Reger took a chair against the wall and realized again how warm the room was. No amount of verbal abuse could be compared to the work outside. *Yes,* he thought to himself, *even a little, puffed-up toad like Herman Boye can be easily tolerated in a room with a stove.*

Three

"Did I not tell you they would give you a new assignment?" Dittner smacked his lips as he tried to use some restraint in gulping down the soup.

"I may even survive this job," Christian mused as he drank his broth slowly. "I'm a payroll clerk for the SS now."

"That's good! Your placement could be of some help to us. But don't underestimate what they will do if you make any mistakes."

"So?" Christian knew how unnecessary the question was.

"Fanaticism has no limits." Dittner set his bowl on the ground. "I saw it again today in the factory."

Reger eyed him as if he didn't really want to hear the story.

"A young Russian, an excellent worker, was assigned to our detail. We all liked him because he had a good sense of humor. Well, as a little joke on one of the men, he incorrectly connected a cable to the engine."

"And they caught him?"

"There had been two cases of genuine sabotage and they blamed everything on him. As we left the factory, they had us watch as they hung him by the neck from one of the gables."

"My, but these Nazis are brave men."

"Now, Reger, let me warn you about something that *will* help you keep your mouth shut and do your work right. Have you heard of Dr. Claus Schilling or Dr. Siegmund Rascher?"

Christian thought for a second. "No, I don't think I've ever heard of them."

"As you work in the office," Dittner carefully instructed, "watch for their names. They are the doctors doing experiments on infirmary patients."

"What have you learned?" Reger stirred uncomfortably.

"Some of the Polish priests have learned that they are using mostly Russians and Poles for their experiments. A Pole told me that they are injecting them with a serum that causes them to become very sick; many have died. Some of the men believe the illness to be malaria. But that isn't the worst part."

"I don't want to know any more." Reger stood to leave. "Enough is enough. I don't want to hear it."

"You must!" Dittner hung onto his sleeve. "None of us may survive this place, but if anyone does, we must not forget anything that happened here. We must remember everything that these maniacs have done."

Christian started to turn away, but then shrugged his shoulders. "All right, what else are they doing?"

"They are dropping men into big basins filled with freezing salt water," Dittner whispered. "Then they try to warm them up to see what happens when people are freezing to death. Most die in convulsions immediately after the experiment."

"How did you find this out?"

"It is hard to muffle screams of pain. But what's important is word has slipped out that Schilling and Rascher are in charge of these debacles. So, watch for their names in the SS office."

Reger nodded his head mechanically.

"Oh, yes, if you ever see either of them, snap to attention and salute. Failure to treat them with special respect can get you a free trip to the laboratory."

"All right, all right," Christian acknowledged. "Let's go back to the barracks."

As they walked along, Dittner observed, "Have you noticed that there are no birds at Dachau?"

"Ya. I've not seen a bird since I came."

"Years ago, this place was a veritable bird sanctuary, but when the smoke began going up, all the birds left." He stopped and pointed ahead. "Look, new prisoners are coming in!"

A new group was moving toward the Jourhaus to be processed.

"I know that man!" Christian exclaimed as he and Dittner got a closer look. "That's Dr. Hermann Hesse! He is a dear friend!"

"Don't yell, for God's sake," Dittner warned. "We'll all be in trouble."

"Dr. Hesse was one of the original signers of the Barmen

Confession. He is a key leader in the Confessing Church."

"I know, I know."

"Look! That's his son Helmut coming through the gate. See how sickly and weak he looks."

Dittner had already started to drop back.

"We must welcome these men," Christian said, trying to wave inconspicuously. "The first hours here are always particularly depressing and hard to bear."

Again Christian tried to get their attention, but when he looked around, Dittner had disappeared.

That night Reger found Dr. Hesse in the back of the Pastors' Barracks. His shaved head, dejected face, and ragged prison uniform made him look like a bundle of misery.

"Dr. Hesse," Christian addressed him respectfully.

The old man slowly looked up and blinked several times as if he were bringing a faraway object into focus.

"Brother Reger!" he exploded. "Brother Reger!" Leaping up like a spry athlete, he grabbed Christian and began hugging him. "Brother Reger! Brother Reger!" he kept saying.

"How can I possibly welcome you to such a place as this?" Christian apologized.

"Ah, it is exactly as in the words of the Apostle Paul, 'My beloved friend, whom I long for, my joy, my crown, stand thus firm in the Lord.'"

"I want you to know that you are among many brothers here. We even have a wonderful bond with the Catholics. I want to introduce you to many of these magnificent men who are my friends."

Dr. Hesse smiled and said, "Oh, I know we are never abandoned. Indeed, even the apostles are a part of this fellowship of suffering. Such pain makes us their contemporaries and they ours."

"Oh, you will do well." Christian shook his hand. "You already possess the real secret of survival that many others here

102

have found. I want you to meet Karl Leisner. He hopes to be ordained as a priest. His faith will encourage you."

Somehow they managed to laugh and shook hands once more.

"I fear most for my son, Helmut. He is very weak. Though I am an old man, my health is much better than his."

Christian immediately began the orientation ritual, warning Dr. Hesse especially about the infirmary. He also told him about the chapel and their worship services.

"You held out a long time," he told Hermann. "How did you keep from being arrested?"

"Because my other two sons and their brother-in-law joined the army, they left us alone. The boys struggled very hard about this matter. None of us felt we should fight for Hitler and were all deeply troubled. Finally, Theodore and Friederich decided the Bible taught they should support the state, so they joined."

"Such decisions are very difficult."

"And now they are both gone." Hermann's voice trailed off. "Theodore died in 1941, and we received word about Friederich earlier this year."

"May God comfort you."

"There is nothing to be said," Hermann said with a quick gesture meant to end any further inquiries and at the same time reassure Christian that he had been consoled. "They were fine Christian men and God has rewarded their faith."

"I want you to know that none of us has shrunk back," he continued. "Helmut has preached astonishing sermons. Even after his brothers' deaths, he accused National Socialism of being a modern Ahab that has turned God's vineyard into a cabbage patch."

"They sent you here because of that sermon?" Christian probed.

"No, there were two other things that finally got us arrested." Hermann stared out the window as if somewhere on the night-time horizon he were replaying a scene from his life. As he looked at that imaginary drama, his whole body seemed to become more erect and strong. "We would do the same again tomorrow!" he said defiantly.

"First, we declared our solidarity with the Jewish people and tried to protect them. Did you notice the big book Helmut brought into the camp?" he asked. "That is a Hebrew Bible. Helmut carries a Torah to show our oneness with all Jews."

"I am amazed that the SS did not take it away from him," Christian observed. "They probably didn't understand what it was and overlooked it. Perhaps it was God's timing."

"God's timing? Ya," Hermann declared, shaking his finger at his Sunday best. "Even in the worst circumstances, I have known God's timing. Indeed, preaching about His timing is the other reason they arrested us.

"Our town of Elberfeld was bombed in a terrible air raid. The next day we held worship services and told the people that the devastation was God's judgment on us for the Nazis' crimes against the Jews."

"I'm sure your arrest came swiftly after that!"

"Oh yes. The police inspector told us that we should be put to the wall and shot. But I would not recant."

His voice fell and the strong emotion was gone. "They put us in solitary confinement for five months with very little food. That is where Helmut became so weak.

"When they arrested us, they took away our Bibles," Dr. Hesse continued. "So, Helmut and I began to write the Bible from memory on scraps of paper we found. We were able to smuggle these verses from cell to cell throughout the whole prison. Once more, God's timing was not thwarted by evil men."

"Ah, Hermann, you are indeed a faithful man," Christian said, squeezing the fellow pastor's hand.

"After three months, they returned our Greek and Hebrew

Bibles. I tell you that it made me rejoice with the psalmist: 'I am jubilant over Thy promise like a man carrying off much booty.'"

"You have an amazing knowledge of the Scriptures," Christian complimented. "You will be of great help to the men here."

"If that is true," he said, grinning and patting Reger's knee, "then once again we have another example of God's timing!

"You know, Christian," Hermann added, "our case went to the highest authorities. Because of the deaths of my sons and my signing of the Barmen Confession, Himmler himself reviewed our files and personally ordered us to Dachau. So you see, we were able to make our witness felt at the very top."

"Nazis at every level of authority have heard the witness of the Confessing Church," Christian said thoughtfully. "God will hold every one of them accountable for all we have seen and heard."

Hermann nodded his head, once graced with magnificent white hair, and looked down at the pitiful rags he was wearing. "This hour is not important, but the day of His judgment and the time of His choosing will be. The Nazis cannot escape any more than did our village of Elberfeld. His timing cannot be defied."

Four

Had it not been for the celebration of the mass in the barracks chapel, Christmas Day at Dachau would have been only another 24 hours of work and exhaustion. Poignant thoughts of home, family, and congregations pressed in upon the men much like the overcrowding. Each wanted the other to be a representation of someone back home who might be praying for him that very night.

Leonard Steinwender carefully opened the worn little Bible and turned to the second chapter of Matthew's Gospel. He began to read of the escape to Egypt of Joseph, Mary, and the Baby Jesus.

"That it might be fulfilled which was spoken of the Lord by the prophet, saying, 'Out of Egypt have I called My Son,' " he concluded, gently closing the book.

"Two things are clear here," Leonard shared in a quiet but fervent voice. "Since this first escape, the child of God has always been in danger in the world."

Immediately, heads nodded to one another. He talked of the ongoing battle with the evil Dragon, then changed direction.

"Second, we can rejoice that the child of God is always saved! Let us never forget that Christ endured the grave; He has overcome this world. Jesus has said to us, 'My peace I give unto you.'

"My friends, we shall be a part of the victory of Christ, and we must see our own exile in that light!" His words were swift and crackled with joyous energy.

At the sermon's close, the pastors knelt on the rough wooden floor to pray. They pleaded for their families and congregations. They prayed aloud for each other and for those in the infirmary lest they be snatched away by the transports.

As Christian's knees bore into the planks, a wonderful discovery began to unfold. He longed for the faces of the people of his parish; and by praying for them, it was as though he once again could visit in their homes and hug their children. His prayer time had become his ministry again and once more he was their pastor. Earnestly, he prayed for their health, their steadfastness, and that the peace of Christ would be real to them.

And he prayed for Mina. She probably was by herself, and he, crammed into a room with many men. Yet they were both utterly alone. He could see her sitting at the kitchen table in their little house, her silhouette illumined by the glow of the fireplace;

and his longing to be with her became almost too great to bear.

Reaching deep into the language of the Spirit, he asked that the promise of comfort be fulfilled for Mina. Almost audibly, he pleaded for the gifts of peace and forbearance to be given to her.

Then warmth began to well up inside him as if to guarantee that the bridge of prayer had crossed the barbed wire and the miles. He knew that he had given her the best gift he could offer on this Christmas.

Slowly but with increasing intensity, emotion swept over him and he began to weep. The sadness, the heaviness, the cruelty seemed to be pouring out through his eyes. Emptiness, loneliness, bitterness seemed to be streaming down his cheeks. For reasons he could not even name, he felt the tears dropping down upon his folded hands.

Yet it seemed that any hate and resentment inside him was being washed away. The more he cried, the more he prayed and the more he prayed, the more he cried. At the end, he could not believe that he was actually praying for the capos, for the guards, and even for Emmerich Ost, the camp commandant. To his own amazement, he was praying that their evil deeds would be forgiven.

He didn't know how he could pray such a thing! It was as though the Holy Spirit had taken over his prayers and was guiding them as He directed. The whole room seemed to glow with peace and goodness.

As Christian rose from his knees, he realized that he had come into this little chapel with even more animosity, resentment, and hatred inside him than he knew was there. The all-encompassing environment of evil had splashed more of its mud and filth on him than he had imagined. Yet now he felt bathed, clean and made fresh inside.

"They cannot make me hate," he thought as he wiped his eyes. "They cannot make me be like them! This place cannot keep me from the joy of Christ."

The words and melody of the first hymn of the evening came back once more—"O Thou loving Jesus Christ, source Thou art of all heaven's bounty." Spontaneously, he reached out to embrace the prisoner standing next to him.

"Peace be unto you," he whispered. "God has given us His own gifts this Christmas. We are under His most special care."

CHAPTER SEVEN   △

SHADOWS
OF DEATH—1943

One

"SUCH A SHORT TIME."

Christian stood silently as the old man rambled.

"I keep reminding myself that I have only been here such a short time." Dr. Hesse thumbed through Helmut's large Hebrew Bible, his head bent, the stubble atop it forming a bizarre pattern. "Yet it feels like a century has passed."

"Ya," Christian reflected. "Time passes like that here. First you measure events by days, then by weeks, and later by months. Now I measure things in years. The flow becomes very twisted."

"I never thought I would outlive all of my sons," Hermann sighed, raising his shaggy white eyebrows very slowly. "But I knew Helmut would not endure in such severe surroundings."

"At least they allowed you to be with him in the infirmary," Christian said, sitting down beside him.

"The last hours were very special and I was comforted. He only awoke twice and his last words to me were, 'O Father!' It was as if he had found a perfect release from all of this misery."

They both slipped back into silence, trying to realize the meaning of the loss of a son. At last, Hermann affectionately laid the Hebrew Bible aside and reached for a German one hidden in the straw of the bed rack.

"A Dutch priest even gave Helmut the last rites of the Roman Catholic Church and then we prayed together," Dr. Hesse reminisced. "I was grateful for such a brotherly gesture."

"Your son was a true martyr, Hermann. God will count him among His special army of saints."

"I thought that very thing the next morning, Christian. When they called me to come and see his body, I reached over and closed his eyelids for the last time. Even in my sadness I realized how very, very proud I was to have known such a fine young man. Though his life was short, he spent it well."

"In these days we have seen uncommon integrity—and you, my friend, have been no less such a person."

"I want to thank you for the flowers that you placed in his hands," Dr. Hesse went on. "In that place of death, your kindness added a remembrance of life."

"I'm sorry I could do no more. I begged the flowers from one of the prisoners who works in the greenhouse."

Hermann opened his Bible to the Gospel according to Matthew. "Helmut loved Hebrew and he knew his languages well. Now in his death, Helmut has given new meaning to the last words of our Lord on the cross—'My God, My God, why hast Thou forsaken Me?' " Then Hermann paused and reread the passage in the original language, "*Eli, Eli, lama sabachthani.*"

"*Sabach-than-i,*" he repeated, emphasizing the "i" and resting his finger on the letter. "That dot on the final 'i' is indeed the axis point around which this whole world turns. Because Christ did not shrink back in His hour of trial, because He endured total abandonment, none of us will ever face death as if we were abandoned. Helmut was not forsaken!"

He closed the Bible with a resounding tone of finality "My

son is gone, but I am most comforted! Our world still turns around that axis."

"The service is about to begin!" someone shouted. "Please gather in the chapel."

As the two men stood up, Dittner appeared in the crowd, moving from man to man, informing each of the service and of other items of news and gossip which he seemed to have the most uncanny ability to gather. As he approached Reger and Dr. Hesse, he reached out to pat Hermann's shoulder in a consoling gesture, then whispered, "The radios are bringing us incredible information! Italy has indeed fallen to the Allies, and apparently we are in deeper trouble in Russia." Immediately he was off again, blending into the multitude that filled the barracks.

"There is much to pray about tonight," Christian told Hermann. "Let me find you a place where you can be close to the front." Knowing of his loss, the group parted before the aging cleric.

Heinrich Gruber stood waiting to preach the evening message. The pastors all knew that when Gruber spoke, his words were laden with power. Opening his Bible to the eleventh chapter of John's Gospel, he began to read, "I am the resurrection and the life; he that believeth in Me, though he were dead, yet shall he live, and whosoever liveth and believeth in Me shall never die."

Out of the corner of his eye, Christian glanced at Hermann's face. He was nodding his head as if he not only agreed with the Scripture passage but was bringing every part of his being into compliance with the words.

Karl Leisner stood next to them. He always seemed to be making mental notes; perhaps he would use the sermon ideas someday when he became a priest.

Heinrich began to talk in quiet, kind tones about Jesus arriving in Bethany to find that His dear friend, Lazarus, was dead. "You see," he said, tapping his Bible with his index finger, "that even in our darkness here in this camp, just as in the darkness of that tomb, the sovereign authority of Christ over death is manifest. Nothing can destroy that power!"

The room was dead silent, though every inch of space was taken by a prisoner. Men leaned forward for fear of missing a word or a phrase.

"Listen to our Lord's sharp words of command as He seizes control of the situation," Heinrich exhorted. " 'Where have you laid him? Take away the stone! Lazarus, come forth!' Jesus is the Master of the moment and all must obey His call."

Then raising his voice as loudly as he dared, Heinrich proclaimed: "The name of Jesus is no empty word! He has won the victory over death and has given us the assurance of eternal life!"

Suddenly from the front door an outsider interrupted the sermon. "Out! Out!" the voice demanded. "Everyone out of the chapel and into the washroom."

Obviously the interruption was timed to disrupt the service. The prisoners groaned as they quickly lined up for another pointless inspection.

"Oh, what marvelous words I have heard!" Hermann repeated as he hung onto Christian's arm. "I cannot say enough praise for what these few moments have given me. Please thank Heinrich for this message about victory over death."

As they shuffled into the washroom, Christian was struck by the fact that not even the planned confusion could diminish the impact that these few simple words had made on him too.

Two

Dittner carefully stepped around the drift to make sure that the snow didn't get inside his shoes. "Have you noticed how our numbers are increasing?"

"And have you noticed how the soup is getting watery again?" Christian remarked, pulling his cap down tightly over his ears. "I told you that would happen."

"The rumors are that Germany is in full retreat."

"Well, at least they released Dr. Hesse. What do you make of that?"

"Considering the broadcasts about Helmut's death, I would guess the Gestapo feared that keeping him here would reveal the full extent of their political arrests. He certainly wasn't freed by accident."

In front of them, multitudes of shivering men were trying to find the right lines and places to stand. Each was waiting as long as possible before having to snatch off his cap and expose his head to prolonged cold.

No. 26 661 conducted an eye search through the ranks to see if any old friends had arrived at Dachau. It had become impossible to keep track of who had disappeared. His gaze fell on Karl Leisner. The deacon was shaking and looked particularly drawn and thin. His face and neck were red with fever.

On this particular morning, several men could not be accounted for, so the guards screamed and shouted, threatened and harassed until the count was satisfied. Finally, the group was released to run back to shelter. At least breakfast was hot.

Following the meal, No. 26 661 hurried to the SS office. Nothing must interfere with his performance lest he find himself back in the fields. As he opened the door, he found the other prisoners already standing at attention, awaiting Boye's instructions before beginning work. To his surprise, a new prisoner had joined their ranks.

When the man turned his head, Christian immediately recognized him as one of the criminals who had been mixed in with the political prisoners. Knoll was widely known as a capo to be avoided; he had a reputation for being violent and explosive. His glance at Christian was less than congenial.

113

"*Seig Heil!*" Boye announced as he entered, extending his arm in a rigid salute. Each man stiffened to attention.

"Unfortunately, you social deviates are not allowed to return the pledge of loyalty to our Führer," Boye said with a smirk as he paced in front of his little company. "Perhaps even now you are beginning to feel some of the pain of being completely outside the circle of socially acceptable human beings. I trust you are learning how important loyalty and fidelity are."

A slight smile inched up the side of No. 26 661's face. Quickly he bit his lip.

The boy officer suddenly whirled and faced his troops. "You can redeem yourselves with acceptable work! Today I expect maximum effort. Some of you have been making mistakes and that will be corrected immediately! I have a report here on you before you have even started," he said, pointing to Knoll. "Any other problem and you go out to the snow!"

The lieutenant thrust a piece of paper into No. 26 661's hand. "Tell this dumb swine how to do things right! Get him straightened up or I'll send both of you back!"

Christian tried to stand even more erect.

"All right! Get to work!" As Boye heeled around and left the room, Knoll turned and faced Christian. He was a hulk of a man, with an enormous neck that ran from the edge of his ears down into the middle of his shoulders. From behind, he had looked like a bull. Now all Reger could see was the defiance and contempt radiating from his deep-set eyes.

"Now, pighead, you are going to set me straight?" Knoll contested.

Christian pretended to be reading the paper. He remembered how Knoll had not hesitated to kill a Jewish inmate and no one had done anything. Maybe killing a cleric would be no different.

"I'm not looking for any trouble," he said without lifting his eyes from the report. "All I can do is follow orders. No harm is intended."

"No harm is intended?" Knoll snarled.

"Of course not," Christian said softly, trying to avoid any further confrontation. "We are all brother prisoners here. Nothing more."

"Oh, I know about you. You are one of those pastors. A *pfaf!*" he huffed, breathing into Reger's face.

The way Knoll said pfaf made Christian realize that he thought that the term was derisive.

"Do you know what a pfaf is?" he asked with as much casualness as he could muster.

The towering convict looked blank for a moment and then answered with surprising candor. "No."

"Pfaf is a Latin acrostic formed by combining the first letters of four words. The phrase is, *Pastor Fidelis Ammarim Fidelium*."

"And what does *that* mean?" Knoll snapped back, waving his thick fist in the air.

"Faithful pastor of faithful souls," Christian answered. "That is all any of us wants to be. Helping others to find God's help is our business."

Again Knoll looked blank and after a moment answered, "Oh, really."

"That's all."

"What are you—some big-deal priest or bishop or something?"

"Oh no, I am a nobody. I'm just a pastor of a little church in Stieglitz, in Pomerania near Poland. I'm nobody special."

"Ya? Then why are you here?"

"I helped organize people into what we call the Confessing Church. We oppose the Nazis and their policies. After I was arrested three times, I ended up here."

"You've been arrested three times?" said Knoll with new respect in his voice. "Well, you must have been pretty powerful in your village."

"No, no," Christian laughed. "No one would ever be afraid of me. The only strength I had was the persuasiveness of truth."

"You had guns and explosives hidden in these churches?"

"Oh no! We didn't operate like that."

"So, why would they bother with you?"

"I suppose that nobodies who won't compromise look very threatening to the people who have the guns and bombs."

Knoll just shook his head. "I've never heard anything like that before."

"Ah, my friend, truth can be a very powerful thing." Christian put his hand on the man's shoulder.

Instinctively, Knoll flinched and drew back. Taking full measure of the pastor, he pursed his lips for a moment, then grunted and turned away.

Reger watched Knoll standing in front of the window waiting for someone to tell him what to do, and suddenly realized he had not said anything to him about what was in the report. However, most of it made little difference and it seemed more prudent to let it pass for now. Later in the day might be a better time to bring it up again.

Three

At first, he only felt weak and his head hurt. Soon after, he became nauseated. "I am getting sick," he told Dittner as they rolled out of the bunks. "I can feel a fever starting to develop."

"Hide it!" Dittner said instantly. "Do everything you can to fight it off."

"I will, I will," Christian assured him. "You *know* I don't want to end up in that infirmary!"

"Ya, and your job is also on the line! Don't let them send you back outside to work."

"Of course not!"

For two days he was able to struggle and keep moving, but as the fever increased, his strength decreased. Finally, he had to face the facts. He had typhus and no matter how hard he tried, it would not go away.

It took great effort to get to the SS office with the cold winter wind blowing down the bunker. He feared the subfreezing temperature would only aggravate his condition.

"Where have you been?" Lieutenant Boye screamed across the office. "I'll teach you to be late!"

Even Knoll looked apprehensive. Christian slowly approached the officer's desk.

"Get that cap off!" Boye screeched. "What do you think we are running here?"

"I'm sorry," Christian mumbled, "but I'm sick. I am late because I keep feeling that I am going to faint."

Boye looked at him skeptically and puckered his lips mockingly.

"However, I didn't want to report to the infirmary without your approval."

"I guess you didn't," the lieutenant mimicked. "Perhaps you need a little fresh air that working in the fields would provide?"

"Oh no, please. I think I have typhus."

"Typhus!" Boye exploded. "Get out of here at once!" he demanded, backing away. "I don't want to catch any of the vile diseases you swine bring in here. Get out!"

"But my work?" Christian feebly protested. "I realize that my work must be done."

"I am ordering you out of here! Don't come back until the fever is gone."

Slowly, No. 26 661 turned and headed toward the door. Knoll gave a subtle but sympathetic nod. Closing the door behind him, he could hear Boye lecturing the men on exposing him to any infections.

As Reger hobbled off to the infirmary, he realized that the

infectious nature of his illness was an ally he hadn't counted on. Boye had given him the official dismissal that he needed to be able to return to work. "Thank God!" he said aloud.

Once a bed had been assigned, he felt an overwhelming urge to sleep. His eyes burned and his head pounded. Within minutes he fell into a deep sleep. Even then, his body shook uncontrollably as the fever rocketed.

"Up! Everybody up!" Christian turned, trying to hide from the sound, yet he could not ignore for long the hand that was roughly shaking him. Finally, he had to open his eyes.

"Out! Everyone outside!" The capo who yelled in his face would obviously tolerate no delays. "Get out, right now!"

His sleep had been so comalike that he had no idea how long he had been there or what day it was. "What is happening?" he sputtered.

"Get up, fool! Everybody is being moved outside. Now, get out of here quickly!"

"Can I dress?"

"Who cares what you have on?" the capo jeered, yanking Reger out of bed and onto the floor. "Outside!"

The transports? The thought was like an ice-cold slap in the face which snapped everything into focus. *Were they loading up the transports? Had he been there that long?* Panic gripped him and he considered running, only to realize he could barely walk. Every ounce of strength was required to get to the doorway.

The icy gusts bit his bare body as he searched for any sign of the large vehicles. To his utter relief, none were in sight. Instead, capos were yelling for the sick to get inside the next barracks. For some reason, they were all changing buildings. As No. 26 661 hobbled to claim a bed, he realized his glasses had been left with his clothes.

"Oh no! My glasses are gone," he pleaded, though no one paid any attention.

Dropping on the nearest bed, he pulled the blankets around

his shaking shoulders. "I must have glasses," he told the man in the bed next to him.

"Open the drawer beside your bed," the patient said, pointing to a little night table. "You will find plenty of spectacles in there. As the men die, the capos just drop their glasses in the drawer!"

To No. 26 661's amazement, the drawer was filled with glasses. He rummaged around until he found a pair that fit quite well.

How grotesque, he remembered thinking as he dropped back into a deep sleep.

When he awoke, light from the window was falling across his face. At first he thought he had only been asleep for a few minutes, yet his body protested. *Surely he must have slept around the clock again.* Propping himself up, he surveyed the room.

The man who had told him of the glasses was lying with his mouth ajar. His glassy stare and ghastly purple color answered any questions about his condition. Here and there across the room Christian could see hands, arms, legs bent at strange angles. There were no nurses, no capos, no doctors. Perhaps the transports would not be needed—the typhus was obviously quite effective. Since prisoners apparently weren't receiving any medicine, it would purely be a matter of how long a man's resistance would last.

The days passed, but no matter how badly Christian feared being swept away in the invalid transports, he couldn't shake the fever. His skin began to slough off, and his mouth felt strange and dead. In horror, he realized he could simply tug on a tooth and it would come out.

"Something is happening to my heart," he told one of the sympathetic capos who finally turned up. "I can feel that it is weakening."

"Be very careful not to exert yourself," the capo warned. "Typhus often damages the heart."

"I can tell there is an insufficiency," Christian said "It scares me." The capo said nothing; both fully understood the implications.

Almost miraculously, the transports did not come. Each morning he prayed for just one more day to recuperate. Perhaps the epidemic had taken a toll of truck drivers. Dittner had smuggled a Bible into the infirmary and he tried to read it as best he could. The capos simply looked the other way when the book appeared. Most of the time he slept.

On one of the empty evenings, a Polish priest beckoned to Christian. The priest's bloodshot eyes and drawn appearance indicated the end had come. He was barely able to prop himself up.

"Plea-s-s-e," he groaned in his thick accent. "Can you help me?"

"Of course!"

"You have Martin Luther Bible?" he asked. "I need Word of God before I die."

Christian crept across the room to the Pole's bedside.

"Our suffering has broken all barriers," Reger whispered to him. "Nothing stands between us. How can I help you?"

"Please read me the Word that gives strength," the priest moaned, putting his skeletal hand on top of Christian's. "Give me word that assures me."

"In the Confessing Church we have lived by this verse. 'We are not among those who shrink back, but who have kept their faith and saved their souls,'" he read. "I know you have not retreated! Believe and have faith. We are not abandoned by God, even in this place."

The priest smiled weakly and patted his hand. "Thank you for kind word. I have tried to be faithful priest."

"Remember," Christian assured him, "if we have lived through hell, then heaven must be very close at hand. Listen to this psalm, 'The Lord is my shepherd, I shall not want; He maketh me to lie down in green pastures. He leadeth me beside the still waters; he restoreth my soul.' "

Christian kept reading long after the priest had closed his eyes. The words seemed to be a soothing lotion for his soul. His hand relaxed; his face became peaceful.

The next morning they carried him out of the barracks. "He was a good man," Christian said to the man in the next bed.

"They are all good men," the raspy voice wheezed.

Christian looked again. The man who had come in during the night was, to his surprise, Camill, the Communist capo who had helped make some of the worship articles for the Pastors' Barracks chapel and had even been in charge of the barracks for a time. The Nazis had hoped his supervision would create tension. Instead, he had absorbed the brotherly spirit.

"Camill!" Christian exclaimed. "How long have you been here?"

"Not long enough," he gasped, trying to sit up. "They would not let me stop work and now it is too late."

He suddenly collapsed on the bed and his whole body went limp. Christian tried to reach him. Camill's eyes slowly opened again.

"I'm sorry," he said, squeezing Christian's hand. "I cannot find it in me to believe in God. I know in this moment you would want me to do so, Reger. But I can't go back on what I believed before I came here.

"I do not believe in angels and I am certainly no hero," he went on, breathing heavily. "But I want you to know I was glad to have been with you. I would wish that all Communists would have a good word for Christians."

"Maybe if I just read a little bit, it would be easier. Would that offend you?"

"No," Camill gently replied. "Please do read out of your Bible."

"Yea, though I walk through the valley of the shadow of

121

death, I will fear no evil; for Thou art with me." Reger continued, finishing the psalm.

When he looked up, the man was dead.

"Only You, O Lord, can be the judge of such things," he prayed. "I commend my brother to You."

Christian managed to get back to bed before once again drifting off into heavy sleep. When he awoke the next day, he realized that his condition had definitely improved. Perhaps the fever had decreased or the hold of the disease had been broken. Whatever the case, he knew the typhus would not kill him now. He began concentrating on getting back to the SS office. As he pondered how much energy he had left, he rubbed his chin and also realized how many of his teeth had fallen out.

Two days later he eased out of the infirmary and back to the office. Just walking across the assembly area seemed impossible, but somehow he mustered the strength.

His first glance at the work station told him Knoll had been promoted to a different desk. The second clarified everything. At least half of the former prisoners were gone.

"Get on with it," Boye ordered, somewhat indifferently. "We're very far behind. Your place is next to Knoll over there." He immediately turned back to his desk as if he had no time to spare, even for lectures.

Sliding in on the bench, Christian watched what Knoll was doing. "What's been happening here?"

"Typhus killed nearly all of them," the hardened inmate grumbled, pushing a pile of papers in front of Christian. "That swine Boye never gets sick!"

Taking the papers, Christian looked out the window in front of them. Cutting across the gray winter sky was the black smoke of the crematoriums. The greasy vapor seemed to be particularly voluminous as it belched up that morning.

"Business seems to be very good these days," he said cynically to Knoll.

When Knoll noticed Reger's gaze out the window, he too watched the smoke curl up to the sky. "I imagine they're behind in processing their claims as well," he snarled. "Well, my fine pfaf, what do you say to all this?"

Christian searched for the right words as he slowly put his response together. "It would seem we have made a descent into hell, wouldn't it?"

Knoll slowly but definitely nodded his agreement.

"Then we must remember that He who first descended also ascended. In His victory He has not abandoned us. We are saved by that hope."

Knoll looked thoughtful. He pursed his lips pensively and then turned back to his papers. For the rest of the morning the two men silently completed the task before them.

CHAPTER EIGHT △

BENT BUT UNBROKEN—1943

One

"WHAT DID SHE WRITE?" Heinrich Gruber pressed forward with the rest of the men. His face was no longer round but oblong. Lines were etched around his eyes, and a great deal of his hair was gone.

Leonard Steinwender leaned closer. "Is she all right? Is Mina well?"

"Yes, yes," Christian assured the entire crowd. His frown betrayed his annoyance at having to share this moment of mail call with a group. Yet how well he felt their hunger for any personal word of warmth from the outside. "Her health is holding up quite well, thank you."

"Are they persecuting her?" some unknown prisoner inquired.

"No, no." Reger shook his head. "That's all past now."

"How does she survive?" the worried-looking unknown persisted, tugging at his sleeve.

"My wife manages on a stipend she receives for playing the

organ in a nearby church." Christian turned his back to the man as he tried to read the rest of the letter privately. Slowly he devoured each phrase and syllable, trying to stretch the small page as far as possible. Finishing, he looked up, only to find that the group was silently waiting for him to share additional details.

"Well," he commenced, addressing his comments mainly to Leonard and Heinrich, "there are not many of the Confessing Church members left in Stieglitz. Mina says that fear has caused most of the people to turn their red cards back to her."

"What are red cards?" the unknown man interrupted again.

"They are the membership cards of the Confessing Church. Things must be getting tougher. It sounds like most of the remaining members have long since scurried for cover."

"Amazing how courage can change with increased cost." Wilhelm Dittner had slipped to the front of the group of prisoners. He gestured with his head to let Reger know he had something to say in private.

"Possibly you might share just a few lines," the annoying prisoner implored. "I have not received any mail since I arrived."

"Please, just a word or two," another man begged.

"Come on, come on!" Dittner tapped his foot impatiently.

Reger surveyed the group and read their stares. Hollow-looking and discouraged eyes, protruding cheekbones, drawn faces He wondered if he looked as bad.

"She writes," and with this he turned back to the first lines on the front side of the page, "that she hopes I get this letter before Christmas. 'My dear husband, it is amazing that another summer has passed and the winter is already upon us. Yet we each have endured and been faithful. Each day I pray for your release and safety!' " He paused, not wanting to share her more personal comments.

"What a wonderful woman!" the persistent prisoner remarked, as if she were a close acquaintance.

"You have been here two, three years?" another man asked.

Christian nodded his head and jumped to the last paragraph. " 'Let us continue to hold to our pledge: we are not among those who shrink back and are lost; we have the faith to make life our own.' " He folded the paper and said solemnly, "Certainly, that is a word for all of us."

Murmurs of approval passed through the group.

"Come on!" Dittner pulled him away from the center of the circle as he nodded to Heinrich and Leonard to join them.

The four men proceeded to the assembly ground where there would be plenty of space between them and the others.

"I have a number of things to tell all of you," Dittner began.

Christian studied his friend's face. He too had the same sunken look about his eyes. A hardness had settled into his features and often something mean seemed to creep across his countenance.

"The radios are confirming our suspicions that the Allied invasions at Normandy were more than successful. Apparently, they are on the move through Europe."

"How do you know?" Leonard sounded dubious.

"We are beginning to get BBC broadcasts, and the Nazi party line has changed. The people are being urged to defend their just victories." Dittner clenched his fist. "God is going to smash them and obliterate the swastika from the face of the earth!"

"All right, all right," Heinrich said calmly. "What else have you learned?"

"For one thing, the crowding and the food supply are going to get even worse. And today we have discovered a new terror to watch for. The nurses and capos in the infirmary have been seen trading bits of gold and now we know why."

"Why?" Christian was hesitant to even ask.

"Ever notice that sick prisoners with gold fillings disappear immediately? People with good dental work die almost before they hit a bed."

The three men shook their heads in disgust and disbelief.

"Things will get worse before they get better," Dittner predicted. "Oh yes!" he added, "I have news that another friend of yours has come in, Christian."

"Who?"

"Ludwig Steil."

"Really!" Christian turned to Leonard and explained, "Ludwig was one of the original signers of the Barmen Confession. He is well known throughout the Confessing Church. In fact, he has been in several jails through the years. I'll find him immediately after supper."

"What there will be of it!" Dittner snorted. "Watch the weather; it will be cold tonight. Warn Steil about getting sick and to get rid of any of his gold-filled teeth."

As Dittner shuffled off to join another group, the three men turned to observe the long line of new prisoners waiting to enter the Jourhaus for processing. "Few, if any of them, will survive *this* winter," Gruber concluded.

The other two men nodded.

Two

For some reason, Ludwig Steil had not been placed in the Pastors' Barracks. When Christian found him, he was sitting at the back of a dormitory filled mostly with criminals and political prisoners.

"Hello, my good brother!"

"Ah, Christian, you are alive!" Ludwig jumped up to embrace him warmly.

Ludwig's once-broad shoulders felt thin and his bones were close to the skin. Christian was shocked to see that he looked as bad as many of the men who had lived at Dachau for several

128

years. Obviously, his treatment in the other Nazi prisons had been brutal.

"The word was slipped to me when they sent you here several years ago," Ludwig recalled. "I often worried and wondered how you had fared."

They sat down on the bed planks and talked about how each had managed to survive. Seeing the grayness in Ludwig's skin and the faded color in his eyes, Christian was impelled to ask, "Do you think you will be able to stand up to being here?"

"There are lice in this bed rack that make it almost impossible to sleep," Ludwig reported. "Of course, the increasing coldness makes it very hard as well. I'm not sure how much strength I have left in me."

"Your health is extremely important to your survival. I must caution you about what can happen in the infirmary."

"I understand. It is the same in all the prisons. My good brother, I no longer worry about living and dying. Somewhere along the way I released that terror. I try to live as honestly as I can in this present moment and I seem to lose track of the rest."

"You have found true courage, my brother!"

"Oh no, certainly not that," Ludwig smiled. "Nothing else is left in me but the necessity of trusting God. 'Give me this day my daily bread' is the only prayer that I have left. His is the only glory that remains."

"I'm sure the days ahead are going to be even harder," Christian told him reluctantly.

"But God is still good!" Ludwig said. "I couldn't sleep last night so I spent the time mentally reviewing all of the Scriptures and songs I knew. What a wonderful way to fill a sleepless night!"

"Ludwig, you are truly a man of God." Christian felt a surge of emotion as he looked at the physically broken human being who radiated supernatural kindness. "It is an honor just to know a person like you."

"No, no," Ludwig half-laughed. "I am only a worn-out vessel whose time is nearly spent. God alone is good and only He is able to make us sufficient for times like these."

"They've bent you, Ludwig, but they will never break you."

"Christian, how often have both of us thought of those words, 'In weakness is His strength made perfect'?" I tell you, I have discovered a secret through all of this. No one deserves the tragedies we have seen, but I know God is not defeated and we shouldn't be either. Every blow they strike has the potential to further perfect our faith and our lives. God will use even their cruelty for our good. We must receive whatever our fortunes with that trust."

"You will be a walking lesson to us all," Christian declared, swallowing the emotion that pressed him. "I came to comfort *you,* and you have encouraged *me.*"

"What is done to us, they must account for, but how we receive it is our responsibility," Ludwig answered.

"My good brother, let me pray for you."

The two men bowed their heads and in the midst of the crowded barracks only one or two noticed or even listened as Christian began. "Gracious Father, we would not have prayed to drink of this cup. Yet as it touches our lips, may You turn the bitterness to blessing and the gall to glory. Be with Ludwig in whatever way can best bring his wonderful spirit to its fullness. Give us courage. Amen."

"And multiply the blessing on Brother Reger," Ludwig added.

Three

"Listen, you worthless wretch!" Lieutenant Boye cursed, and slammed the pile of papers in front of Reger. "I want this work done by tomorrow night or I'll put you out there with the snow commando!" He had lost his sophisticated air and no longer seemed boyish. He appeared on the verge of hysteria.

No. 26 661 nodded his head vigorously.

"Don't give me that arrogant look that you money-grabbing holy men like to use on the ignorant and illiterate!"

Again No. 26 661 said nothing, only lowered his eyes. His face showed no emotion. Across the room, Knoll turned and leered at the back of the lieutenant.

"We should have shot you high-and-mighty religious traitors in the beginning." Boye put his mouth against the prisoner's ear and shouted, "Get it done or out you go!" His usually fastidiously combed hair fell into his eyes.

He spun on the heels of his black boots and stomped across the room. The door slammed behind him with a thundering echo.

"They're losing," Knoll jeered, "and he's unraveled today." The burly man stole across the room to Reger's desk. "You bother him because you don't crack or show anger. He doesn't know what to do with you."

No. 26 661 only smiled. How personable and warm his incorrigible colleague had become!

"The rest of us always have hate or terror in our eyes. Boye knows what to do with that. But you don't have the look. That eats our little Nazi toy soldier alive."

"Let's just make sure I get this work done lest I give him some excuse to carry out his threat."

"Absolutely!" Knoll wrinkled his brow and looked concerned. "We can't let anything happen to you—that's for sure!"

The outside door at the end of the corridor opened and shut quickly. Dittner tapped his feet against the wall to get the snow off and came down the hall.

"What are you doing in here?" Reger looked at the opposite door, fearing that Boye would come back.

"Who's this?" Knoll's whole countenance changed, and once again viciousness was in his eyes.

"He's a friend," Christian assured him. "You'd better get to your desk or Boye will think we're all plotting something."

As Knoll returned to his work, Dittner bent over the table in front of Reger. "I have been sent to deliver this from the factory to the salary office," he said very loudly and officially. Then he added in an almost inaudible whisper, "The papers have been smuggled in. The documents from Cardinal Faulhaber and the Bishop of Münster have arrived to validate Karl's ordination. Almost no one knows of this, and it must be kept secret."

Christian acknowledged his message without making a sound. Knoll continued to work, not seeming to eavesdrop.

"What an irony!" Dittner continued to whisper. "The Gestapo arrested the one person needed to complete the ordination! When I heard that the Bishop of Clermont Ferrand was here, I knew God had arranged to fulfill Karl's dreams."

"When will it happen?"

"Tonight. If Karl is well enough, the ordination will be tonight."

"Wonderful!" Reger was so loud that Knoll turned around and frowned at him.

"Even the ordination vestments have been completed and smuggled into the barracks. Now I am here because they want your help."

"Of course! Certainly!"

"Because you have access to the small kitchen in this building, the bishop hoped you might prepare a little something as a banquet supper for our new priest."

"It would be a great honor, but there certainly isn't any food around here," Christian said, motioning with his thumb toward the bare cupboards in the other room.

"We all know it would be only symbolic," Dittner assured him, "but it would fulfill the traditional expectation for the way in which a new priest is honored." Without giving Reger a clue as how to find food, he added, "One more thing—Ludwig Steil has taken a serious turn for the worse. He wants to see you."

Reger made no reply. His mind was already at work trying to find some way to provide the ordination banquet.

Since it was well past the usual time to close the office and Boye had not returned, the three men decided to leave. After all, no one had an excuse to miss the roll call.

"If there's some problem and you need help with anything"— Knoll crinkled his nose and showed his teeth—"you let me know."

"Thanks, my friend, but I'm sure everything will be all right."

The men nodded and parted in different directions. To his surprise, Christian immediately saw a prisoner who worked in the greenhouse coming past him on his way to the mess hall. He was carrying a basket filled with brussel sprouts.

"Hey, friend, I have something for you."

The prisoner eyed him suspiciously and barely slowed down. "And so does every other starving swine I've passed in the last five minutes. Keep away from the basket."

"All I need is two or three of the sprouts," No. 26 661 said, falling in beside the man.

"You grab any and I'll turn you and your number in to the nearest guard," the man wheezed. "If I show up with an empty basket, I'm dead! So keep away."

"All right, all right, I will pay you something."

The man stopped abruptly. "I can sell you four and no more. What have you got?"

"Well, ah, well," Christian was fighting for time, trying to think of some source of barter. "What will you take?"

"You got money, cigarettes, maybe chocolate?"

"I'm sure I can get some. Give me some time."

"Are you crazy? You either got it now or you can forget it." The prisoner started to pull away.

"No, please wait!" Christian got a firm grip on his sleeve. "Look, I'm a clergyman in the Pastors' Barracks and something very important is about to happen."

"Ya, ya." The prisoner seemed more amiable. "I know about you and the priests over there and I know about the good you do. But people are starving all over this place. If someone's going to chance eating stolen food, it might as well be me."

"No, no," Christian begged him. "That's not it. A very special event is going to happen right under the nose of the Gestapo and this food is needed to help make it occur."

"Really?" The man sounded skeptical, but intrigued. "Tell me what it is."

"Honestly, I can't, but I promise I will somehow get payment back to you for the sprouts. I promise it on my oath of ordination."

The prisoner eyed his basket thoughtfully. "I keep my mouth shut very well. It sounds to me like you need my help. So . . . ." His stare communicated he would do nothing until he heard the secret.

"No one must know until it's done." Christian's eyes darted back and forth as he tried to make the right decision. He bit his lip, struggling with each word. "You must swear to God on the penalty of your immortal soul not to tell anyone until much later."

"I will. I will," the man agreed, grinning like a naughty boy getting in on a prank. "I promise not to talk. Now, what is it?"

"We are going to ordain a priest right under their noses! We've outwitted them in every way and I need the sprouts for the new priest's banquet."

"Really!" The man smiled broadly. "Amazing!"

"You must not tell," Christian warned.

"Listen, I'm here because I'm a thief and a liar and I know it. But I still believe. Maybe I haven't done much that's worthwhile in my life, but I'd give anything to watch that happen!"

134

He reached into his basket and began putting sprouts in Christian's pocket. Here are six they'll never miss. Cook 'em slow and carefully."

"How much do I owe you?"

"Nothing. Just remember me when you are next on your knees." Quietly, the prisoner moved away and broke into a trot to compensate for his delay getting to the mess hall.

Christian almost danced with jubilation. *How appropriate that a Dachau ordination supper be prepared from food snatched from the Nazis' garbage,* he thought. *Certainly, the prisoners don't get such delicacies.*

Later, as darkness covered the camp, a small group of clerics assembled outside the Pastors' Barracks to stand guard and watch the ordination procession enter the chapel.

"The ring and the cross are already inside!" Dittner beamed. "They were made in the Messerschmitt factory right under the guard's nose!"

His frosty breath reminded Christian how cold it was standing in the snow. He rubbed his arms trying to keep warm.

"A Trappist monk was able to make a crosier," Dittner continued. "And the cardinal sent the ordination oil. The guards never caught a thing."

They saw the door open in the barracks across the way and Karl came out with two men on each side. Obviously, they were making sure he did not stumble and fall.

"Congratulations! God bless you." Christian put his arms around Karl's rickety shoulders and hugged him. "You have made it!"

The deacon smiled very kindly, returning the hug, then shaking Dittner's hand.

After the other priests had escorted Karl into the Pastors' Barracks, Christian turned to Dittner and confessed, "I fear the tuberculosis is too advanced for him to recover."

"But after tonight, it will never matter. He will die a priest and that will be sufficient for Karl."

The snow started to fall more heavily and the wind began to blow. They began stomping their feet to keep them from going numb.

"He will die a priest and a brave man who was faithful," Christian added. "Few have ever done more, and it will indeed be enough."

He watched the snow swirl and decided it was time to begin cooking the brussel sprouts still hidden in his pocket.

When he returned with the little covered dish, the ceremony was already completed and the men were standing around the newly robed priest, who was seated at a table.

"Ah," the bishop welcomed Christian's entry, "here is our banquet for Father Leisner."

Reger quickly set the dish on the table and pushed it toward Karl. He stepped back, smiling with total delight.

"Now let us bless what God has provided." The bishop gave the blessing and ended with the sign of the cross.

Karl kept smiling and expressing an embarrassed appreciation for all the attention he was receiving.

Handing him a fork, Christian asked, "May I see your ordination ring?"

The machine-tooled ring shone on his thin hand.

"It looks perfect!" Christian complimented, then announced so all could hear, "We have confirmation that the everlasting arms are still holding strong!"

"Hear! Hear!" echoed around the group in a simulated toast.

One of the priests held the crosier as Karl bent over the dish. His regal vestments struck a strange contrast with the other prisoners' uniforms and recycled clothes; so too with the starkness of the room. The garments seemed obviously alien, yet hauntingly appropriate.

"Who could ever believe that here in Dachau we would have witnessed such a triumph of the Gospel?" one priest asked

136

another. "The power of the Cross remains hidden but undiminished!"

The group gathered around the new priest, making congratulatory comments as he ate the little cabbages. They laughed and enjoyed the moment as if a pope were being crowned. Yet each of them could hardly keep from noticing how the fork trembled in his bony fingers.

"Please forgive me," Karl finally said. "I think I must lay down now. I feel very faint."

"Of course, of course!" several men responded.

"We will celebrate your first mass tomorrow," the bishop consoled. "Then you will have your full strength back."

Everyone agreed and two priests helped Karl to his feet and back to bed. Everyone knew it would be several days before he could carry on.

"You have been here for many Christmases, Reger?" the bishop queried as Karl left.

"Ya, this is my fourth Christmas here," Christian told him. "Although it has been barren, each year God has been good and given me a special gift."

"How interesting," the bishop answered thoughtfully. "I think this year He has already given me a very important gift."

"Oh? What is it?"

"I have never known what brothers I had among the Protestants! Karl has told me how you have cared for him and been concerned for his welfare. You have been like a shepherd to him."

"You would have done the same for us," Christian pointed out.

"I was raised solely with Catholics," the bishop continued. "Now I know how much I have missed. Truly, Christ has made us to all be brothers."

"If we live," said Christian, extending his hand, "we must never forget this gift."

The bishop suddenly went past the outstretched hand and hugged Christian as one does when being reunited with a long-lost relative. "Tonight the body of Christ has been manifested in our midst. We have been one in Him."

Christian smiled widely. "Let us pray that Karl can consecrate the mass on Christmas Day. That would make the gift complete."

Four

Ludwig Steil's condition had indeed worsened.

"Thank you so much for coming," he said, gripping Christian's hand. "I am not doing very well today."

"Typhus is hard to defeat," Christian acknowledged. "But by God's grace I defeated it last year. You can do the same."

"I'm afraid my time is spent. I'm just too weak."

"No! You must never say that! You must not give up. Dying is God's business. Living is our business!"

"All right," said Ludwig in a surprised tone. "All right, I will keep trying."

"Tonight is Christmas Eve, Ludwig. Wonderful things happen on this night and they are happening here. This is not the time to give up hope."

"Christmas Eve!" Ludwig sighed. "Memories alone ought to strengthen us."

"I am going to bring the evening message tonight and lead the pastors in prayer. Do you have any message you would like me to bring them from you?"

Ludwig closed his eyes as if he were spiritually searching his mind and heart for some special word. "I think," he pondered aloud, "that I would want to bring back to mind Psalm 50:2-3. I believe that text says, 'Out of Zion, the perfection of beauty,

God hath shined. Our God shall come, and shall not keep silence.' "

Christian was amazed at Ludwig's memory, even under such arduous conditions. "That is, indeed, a word from the Lord! You have confirmed what was going through my own mind. Bonhoeffer once wrote something to the effect that no one can possess God in such a way that he no longer needs to wait for Him. In fact, when we wait for God, it is only because God Himself has already been waiting for us for a long time."

"So!" followed Ludwig, waving a finger in the air, "we are waiting for the One who is already on His way!"

"Now," Christian sternly but lovingly admonished him, "you keep on thinking up sermons and quit thinking bad thoughts about your health!"

"I will be incurably a preacher to the end," Ludwig admitted with a grin.

"So it seems, so it seems," Christian laughed.

Once more they clasped hands and prayed together.

In a few minutes, Reger was back in the Pastors' Barracks. Though the electricity had already been shut off for the night, candles lit up the chapel, emitting an almost unearthly glow as they reflected in the faces of the men. The prisoners huddled together more like a pack of ragged beggars than men of the cloth. Yet there was no shoving or pushing. A courtesy prevailed that seemed foreign to a room full of hungry, tired, dispossessed victims of a maelstrom.

Opening his fraying Bible, Christian read the Scripture Ludwig had suggested, then preached, "We would appear to be the prey of the Beast that has pulled us, beaten and broken, to the Dragon's den. But the darkness has not been able to extinguish the truer light and it has not quenched His radiance on this Christmas Eve. Let me tell you what I see as I look into this dark night."

He reflected on Karl's ordination, the bishop's insights, and his own time with Ludwig. Men nodded their heads, murmured their affirmation, and found encouragement and hope. Then they all prayed together, "Come quickly, Lord Jesus."

As the worshipers filed back to their bed racks, Christian lingered in the chapel. His last prayers were that Mina, as on other Christmases, would be comforted and would have some realization that he was alive, surviving, and spiritually with her. He prayed until an inner confirmation allowed him to arise and return to the dormitory. Wedged between two friends, sleep quickly overcame him.

It was not until the day after Christmas that Karl was finally strong enough to celebrate his first mass. So many prisoners were packed into Dachau that the guards had come to pay little attention to the frequency of the services in the Pastors' Barracks. In fact, they seemed to have their hands full in just maintaining the camp.

Karl was almost overwhelmed at the attention being shown him. By the time of the service, everyone knew of the ordination and considered him a walking symbol of hidden victory. The fact that he was so sick seemed to strengthen the resolve of the others.

To the amazement of everyone but Dittner, a camera appeared. Behind locked doors, pictures were taken of the new priest in his makeshift vestments. The camera was then carefully smuggled away to make sure Karl's family would have proof and remembrance of his ordination and first consecration of Communion.

"Please come in the chapel and stand with us," Karl told Christian. "The service would not be complete without you."

The bishop smiled and motioned his approval.

Karl carried himself with natural priestly bearing. While he had often seemed awkward and unable to do the work in the fields, now he slipped smoothly into the place for which he had been destined. Even the crude, handmade utensils of worship received a new dignity at his touch.

His simple homily, purified through the pain of imprisonment, demonstrated a spiritual maturity that years of study could not match. Leaning on the table for support, he began to speak of the holy family and the shepherds on the first Christmas.

"Did they not celebrate His nativity in a poor barn in an occupied country? Here we have been given a privilege that few can know. Like them, we have been reduced to being the poorest of creatures. Yet God's grace used their poverty as His opportunity. Even the treachery of Herod was thwarted. At that moment they could not see God's plan that would only be understood from distant and later years.

"Our pain and poverty will ultimately be His opportunity. Let us hold to our faith and not retreat. Let us have the faith to make life our own. Amen."

Karl turned to move the little wooden chalice to the center of the table. *How much that chalice must look like the true grail,* Christian thought.

The priest's eyes sparkled as he elevated the cup. No longer did he look weak and sickly; rather, his face was serene and confident. For a moment he kept the chalice aloft. And in that moment, it seemed as if all questions of power, authority, and destiny were settled.

CHAPTER NINE △

THE FINAL CALDRON OF PAIN—1944

One

THUNDEROUS EXPLOSIONS SHOOK the ground; sounds of terror rang through the night air. Somewhere, off in the distance, terrible destruction was falling from the sky.

The prisoners watched the Allied bombers flying toward the ammunitions factories located around Munich. Huddling in the darkness, each man wondered if the torture he had survived through the years at Dachau would be ended by a stray bomb that might hit the camp.

When the newer prisoners admitted their fears, Christian told them the story of the matchbox that had been smuggled into Schneidemühl prison and how it had been an illumination that dispelled the shadows of his despair. Again and again, he shared the lessons he had learned in the furnace of adversity.

"Don't let the unseen terrify you," he comforted. "Keep remembering the words of the psalm, 'The Lord is the light of my life.'"

With the first light of day, the SS guards usually selected some of the prisoners as death squads to search for stray, unexploded bombs. The rest trudged off to roll call and then to their jobs.

"No. 26 661!" Lieutenant Boye snapped. "You're to see the doctor."

Christian's head jerked up from his work. "I'm not sick. I have not requested any medical attention."

"Nobody asked you!"

A frantic sensation surged through Reger's body. "I would respectfully decline this attention, Sir."

"Get to the infirmary!" the officer demanded. "And don't waste any time getting back here."

Dropping his pencil, Christian reluctantly headed out the door.

Why would a physician want to see me? he thought. No one ever received special care unless a sinister purpose was behind it. Christian worried about the few teeth he had left, then remembering he had never been able to afford gold fillings, his mind quickly leaped to the secret experiments. Perhaps he had offended someone in the pay office and his name had been turned in. Was he to be disposed of in the guise of "special care"?

"O Lord," Christian prayed softly as he waited in the corridor, "please don't let this doctor be either Schilling or Rascher."

Then an unusual thought struck him. *Today is Pentecost Sunday, 1944! This is the day when the Holy Spirit empowered the church. He will indeed be with me today!*

"Come in, come in," a kindly voice beckoned.

Looking up from his reflections, Christian was relieved to see an unfamiliar face.

"I am Doctor Klaus," he introduced himself. "I have especially asked to see you." Smiling and extending his hand, he motioned the prisoner into the examination room. "I want to make sure you are well," he said pleasantly.

No. 26 661 watched in amazement as the doctor listened to his heart and examined his chest.

144

"My daughter-in-law asked me to look in on you," he said very quietly. "She is a good friend of your sister and they are all concerned for you."

The kind manner and concern almost overwhelmed Christian. "Oh thank you, thank you," he said, gripping the doctor's hand with deepest appreciation. "Please, let my sister know I am surviving."

"Well," he said slowly, staring at Reger's protruding ribs, "you are surviving, but I'm sure you know that your health is very bad. Nonetheless, your constitution is still strong."

"I hope to be released some time soon," Christian answered, fishing for some response from the doctor.

"I hope you are no longer set on any resistance to our Führer," he said sternly. "We are in a new day now. Those who recognize the glory of National Socialism can find their place in the new order."

Reger wasn't exactly sure what was being suggested, but the response the doctor wanted from him was obvious. Perhaps the right political statement might make a difference. Maybe repentance would even win his release.

His eyes glazed over and he had no idea how long he thought about his answer. Mina's face came to mind and he could see the parish church almost as if he were standing before it. The years at Dachau had been so, so long.

And then he began to see other faces—Werner Sylten, Van Mohl, the dying Polish priest, and finally, Helmut Hesse lying with Reger's flowers in his hands. The gypsy's description of Paul Schneider's death also was resurrected in his memory. *No, he reluctantly thought to himself, we have all come too far to shrink back now.*

"New?" Christian answered the doctor. "No, I do not see new things growing up around me. Let me ask you a question. Do you know what today is?"

Looking perplexed, the doctor shook his head.

"Today is Pentecost. This day was the only time when something truly new and hopeful happened. All the other comings and goings of men and governments are not new. None of them will last forever. Let us not deceive ourselves about what shall remain."

The doctor stiffened and stepped back. His eyes narrowed and he looked at Reger with disgust. Pointing the patient toward the door, he abruptly said good-bye.

A sinking feeling swept over Christian as he watched the little oasis of hope fade back into the desert of despair. The brief interlude of promise dissolved into a mirage. "Another day, perhaps?"

The doctor said nothing.

Two

"Good Lord!" Heinrich Gruber exclaimed as he stamped his feet. "This room is crawling with lice! They are everywhere!"

"It's even worse in some of the other barracks," Dittner reported.

"What's made the lice suddenly become so much worse?" Christian asked.

"The transports from the Balkans are bringing in so many people that there is no way to disinfect them," Dittner said, slapping at his arm. "These barracks are jammed to overflowing. One barracks built for 200 has 1,600 prisoners."

"I saw the clothing piles of these new prisoners yesterday," added Gruber. "The lice were so thick that the heap was actually moving!"

"I talked with the capo who is responsible for disinfection," Dittner continued, "and he said there are simply not enough

146

chemicals to control the vermin. It's certain that typhus will once more rage through the camp."

"Perhaps this time none of us will survive," Christian said blankly, almost casually, about death's constant presence.

"Possibly our contact with typhus last year will have built up some immunity," Gruber suggested hopefully. They all shrugged their shoulders.

As the days passed, rest and sleep became almost impossible. The attack of the lice was unrelenting. Soon men fell ill and could not leave their block beds; excrement fell down on those below and yet nothing happened. More prisoners just kept piling in.

Trying to find fresh air, Christian and his friends left the barracks and began watching new prisoners being herded into the Jourhaus. A change was evident in the long lines. These were not inmates from the north or even from Russia; these were clearly German citizens.

"These are our good fellow-citizens," Dittner growled. "They would not stand with us in '33 or in '38, and now they are paying the price for their cowardice!"

"None of them will speak of it for fear of their lives," Steinwender mused, "but the word is out. Because of an attempt on Hitler's life, thousands are being sent here."

"They have it coming! And I hope they taste the full, bitter cup extended to them in this place!" Dittner ground his fist into his palm.

"Is that the best we have learned here?" Christian questioned, looking Dittner squarely in the eye. "Are we to be consumed by the same hate that drives this place and fuels its fires?"

"The subject is so sensitive no one dares mention the assassination attempt," Dittner went on, avoiding Christian's eyes. "But they *will* say that the war is going very, very badly."

"More tents will be required now that the barracks can hold

no more," said Leonard. "The only place left to put them is on the streets and walkways."

"Look!" Christian pointed to a prisoner trotting across the open square. The man had his hand over his mouth and was bent forward.

"That's Father Goldschmitt!" Steinwender exclaimed. "His work is unloading the trains."

"Unbelievable, unbelievable," the priest was muttering as he approached. "It's unbelievable."

"What's happened?" Dittner wanted to know.

"I can't comprehend it." His face was ashen and he seemed to gag on his own words.

"They were unloading two trains from Compiegne—all Frenchmen."

"What? What?" Dittner interrogated in his relentless way. "What did you see?"

"Piled in those cattle cars were 370 bodies," the priest said, putting his hand to his mouth. "Scattered among the dead were the living. I cannot even describe the stench!"

"Do you know how they died?" Dittner persisted.

"I'm sure it was from hunger, thirst, and the heat," Goldschmitt answered, slapping at the lice working underneath his shirt. "I saw the information sheet on the train. Twenty-five hundred men had been loaded into those cars in France. But when they arrived here, there were only 950 left alive."

"Do the guards know that you read the count?" pried Dittner.

"I'm afraid so," Goldschmitt said. "But they told us that the other dead had been unloaded along the way. The Gestapo said that they fought among themselves and ended up trampling each other to death."

"Did you let them think you believed that?" Dittner urged.

"Of course!" the priest assured them. "But I know the truth. Most of those men actually suffocated to death."

For a moment, they stopped talking and once more beat their clothing to kill the lice that seemed to be in every possible place.

Then suddenly, Goldschmitt began to shout at the top of his voice, "Germany can never make amends for this! God will not let this stand!"

Instantly, they realized that he had lost control. If anyone heard him, the penalty would be swift and severe. Together, they tried to silence him as best they could.

Sandwiching the sobbing priest between Dittner and Reger, the men ushered him back to the barracks. Though they knew the lice would give him no peace, they stretched Goldschmitt out on one of the bed racks.

"He simply has seen too much," Steinwender sighed. "There is a breaking point for all of us."

As they bent over the priest, a prisoner pushed his way through the crowded room and walked up to Dittner. Cupping his hand to Dittner's ear, he whispered something that caused Wilhelm to jump in excitement. He slapped the man on the back and the other inmate disappeared from sight. Father Goldschmitt became silent and motionless.

"If we can keep healthy and out of trouble, we may yet make it!" Dittner assured the little group. Then pulling them closer together, he said quietly, "The Allies have taken Paris and are moving across France."

"Ah!" Gruber said enthusiastically, "this will put new pressure on the government. They will have to do something about Dachau now."

"Pressure?" Christian responded. "Yes, but pressure to do what?"

"They will have to release us if the Allies come close enough to our borders," Gruber insisted.

"No," Christian said very flatly. "They will not have to release us at all. In fact, if the tales of what we have seen here are ever told, the SS and National Socialism will be indicted for the rest of human history. If Heinrich Himmler personally knew about Hermann Hesse's case, do you think he will let all of this cruelty come back to convict him?"

"But what else would they do?" a new prisoner eavesdropping at the edge of the circle asked.

Christian looked at his healthy face that had not yet tasted the full wrath of the winter wind and remembered himself as he had been four years before. Through the window he could see the smoke and fire still belching up from the chimneys.

"Never forget which way the wind blows here," he told the nameless face. "That smoke is the primary fact of life here."

"Well, well," Dittner chided. "After all of these months you have finally come to think like me." Turning to Gruber he added, "Now it is *your* turn to learn to read correctly the signs written in the clouds."

"I don't think like you at all!" Christian answered harshly, attending once more to Father Goldschmitt.

Three

Each day the reports from the hidden radios kept coming in increasing crescendos of excitement. In September, Brussels was liberated, and a few days later Holland was free of Hitler's control. When Christian heard that Amsterdam was freed, he remembered Van Mohl and the day he died. "He would have been overjoyed at this news," he thought to himself.

The arrival of new prisoners increased too. Since summer, the influx of "special action" prisoners was especially heavy. These were men who had been suspected of having some part in the assassination attempt on Hitler. Without any background of enduring hard winters and fighting off terrible infections, this group fell very quickly to the typhus that thrived on the ever-present lice.

So many died so fast, bodies were left to pile up between the barracks. Even the SS guards began to show a marked loss of morale. Perhaps Hitler had been told of the need to encourage his loyal guards. Whatever the reason, in November, 1944, it was rumored he was coming to Dachau.

"Attention, attention!" Lieutenant Boye shouted through the SS office. "I have wonderful news for everyone!"

Both officers and capos stopped their work and looked up. Boye was holding a communiqué in his hand and waving the papers in the air.

"Our glorious Führer is coming to visit us!"

The officers enthusiastically applauded; the prisoners weren't sure of an appropriate response.

"We must make this office a model of efficiency and show the Führer the high quality of service performed here at Dachau!" Boye preached like an evangelist.

The lieutenant marched around the room, firing off orders and instructions as to how special details were to be handled. Each SS official seemed to be completely recharged with energy and excitement. Turning his back on the office group so only Reger could see him, Knoll contorted his face in mock rage and gestured obscenely. Watching Knoll's antics while looking across his shoulder at Boye's was so comic Christian had to bite his lip for fear he would laugh and be in serious trouble.

"Of course, none of you swine will be allowed to be part of this glorious day," Boye spouted, and flipped his hand as if to wave the prisoners away. "You will be confined to the barracks and if there are any problems, trouble will be annihilated in an instant!"

As the afternoon progressed, Christian was amazed to observe how Hitler's approaching arrival seemed to fuel the Nazis' fanaticism. The whole experience felt like preparation for a high moment of religious worship.

The bleakness of the camp began to change dramatically. Red and black swastika flags were unfurled everywhere, formal uniforms appeared; by the end of the day, soldiers with rifles were goose-stepping up and down the streets. Over and over again, the guards made it abundantly clear that the slightest irregularity among the inmates would be met with violent response. Absolute security was to prevail!

The next morning, long before Hitler's motorcade arrived, a brass band began to blare the German national anthem, then went from one furious march to another. Trumpets and bass drums echoed from every corner of Dachau.

"He is here! Hitler has arrived!" swept through the barracks. "Satan is in our midst!" one priest whispered in the subdued dormitory.

Like a strange holiday of silence, the day passed quietly for the prisoners. While the bands blasted away, they sat silently on their bed racks, soberly listening to the celebration. At least they were not being worked! As the day faded, so did the sounds. By evening, the gray shroud of agony was again drawn over the camp.

The morning after, Boye paced up and down the office corridors. Walking among the rows of desks like a man whose wife had just given birth to a son, he kept describing aspects and memories of Hitler's visit over and over again.

"The propaganda of our enemies cannot keep us from the truth," he announced smugly to Christian. "I heard the Führer himself say that we are winning!"

Turning to another SS guard, he continued, "Did you notice how strong the Führer was? He was more vigorous than ever before! The attack on his life did nothing to him."

The office functionary emphatically agreed.

"He told me *personally*," Boye continued, with an arrogance that was so obvious that even the SS men must have been repulsed, "that our work here is of the utmost importance to the Reich!"

The lieutenant suddenly pointed his finger at Reger. "We are upholding the truth for *all* Germany. You clerics could never comprehend the liberation we are bringing to the multitudes that the churches once kept captive with their delusions and lies. We will prevail because we are right."

Christian looked straight ahead, portrait still.

"Hitler told us in the most vivid terms that it is now our moral duty to defend the Fatherland in this hour of unjustified attack on our very soil. He also shared with us how secret weapons are about to be unveiled that will sweep away the adversary in a burst of flames. This is a great hour for all courageous men!"

"We are living in a glorious hour!" one of the SS guards chimed in. "Only fools cannot recognize what is happening."

Knoll and Reger began dusting the furniture, ignoring the obvious inference. *Only fools cannot recognize the hour*, Christian thought to himself. *So* you *say!*

Four

The deafening roar shook the whole building and the accompanying explosion turned the black night into day for a brief moment. Men tumbled out of their beds and scrambled for the windows. Pressing against the panes, they could see fires burning along the horizon, only a few kilometers away.

"What's going on? Why the fires? Are those bombs?" Questions buzzed through the barracks. Ten minutes later, everyone knew the answer.

"We are being bombed! What an irony!" Christian told a

friend. "This morning Boye assured me they were winning. Tonight the first bombs fall on us!"

"This is just the beginning," another prisoner added. "Surely the Messerschmitt factory and the munitions plants we work will be prime targets for air raids."

The next morning Dittner brought radio word that the Russians were in East Prussia. "Oh no!" Christian exclaimed. "My wife is near there!"

Karl Leisner gripped Christian's wrist, trying to buoy him, but the new priest broke into one of his coughing spells.

"No, no," Gruber warned Reger. "Do not let your mind think about such things. Just keep praying for her protection. Fasten your mind onto the promises that have sustained us thus far."

"You have trusted God to save *you*," Dittner assured Christian in an unusually kind way. "Now trust Him to save *her*."

The emotional agony seemed worse than any he had known before. He knew he had to remember that if God was keeping him alive, He could certainly sustain Mina. Nevertheless, the pain of helplessness cut through his very soul.

As friends gathered around to pray for Mina, guards broke into the room screaming. "Out of here! Everybody out of here!" The prayer circle was scattered. "We are going to clean up you pigs, once and for all!"

"To the showers!" capos and guards bellowed.

Out of the barracks, inmates tumbled into the lanes. They were being herded toward the showers next to the crematoriums. Clubs and whips were swung through the air as the screaming continued. "Faster! Faster!"

"The showers!" Gruber gasped as he hurried to keep step. "That's how they have been gassing people!"

"No! No!" Dittner protested. "It can't be. We have had those showers sabotaged. It isn't possible that they have been able to hook up gas to run through them"

"Then what are they doing?" asked Christian.

"Perhaps this *is* the end," another prisoner said stoically.

When they turned the corner, each could see that the men ahead were taking off their clothes.

"Strip! Everybody strip!" the guards yelled at each group.

"What? The temperature is below freezing," one of the men yelled back.

Immediately, the guard hit him across the face with a club. The prisoner dropped to the ground with a sickening thud. After kicking him in the stomach, the guard pushed him into the ditch.

"Anyone else have hearing problems?" he barked. Instantly, clothes began dropping in piles.

The word that they were being disinfected for lice passed through the line. "This is not extermination!" spread from man to man.

Yet as Reger shivered in the cold, he wasn't sure there would be any difference. The sick—in the same naked condition—were obviously going to die from extended exposure. Around him, those who didn't make it were being carted away in wheelbarrows.

For fourteen hours, the process continued without break. There was no food and nothing to drink. Those who didn't move quickly enough into the showers were thrown bodily into the tanks. Some were simply dropped into the disinfecting tanks and left there. By the end of the day, the body count had reached a new high.

About 8 o'clock, they were sent back to the barracks. Many of the men had even walked through the snow in their bare feet.

"Be grateful that we have tried to end the typhus epidemic," the capo snarled as they arrived at the barracks. "You priests and preachers ought to be in that chapel of yours thanking God for such good care."

A French priest huddled next to Reger in the crowded beds.

The snow was blowing in through the broken window. "They are desperate," he said. "They know the end is not far away and they amuse themselves with such tortures. Perhaps God will use this day to save some men while hastening the end of those prisoners whose condition is hopeless."

"The end is not far away," Dittner confirmed. "The Allies are not far from the Rhine River."

"I must see to Ludwig Steil," Christian coughed. "I do not see how he could survive today."

"Be careful walking around in the dark," Dittner warned. "The guards are getting very edgy."

When Christian found Ludwig, the perspiration was beaded on the sick man's flushed forehead. His body was limp, his eyes glassy.

As Christian reached for his head, Ludwig's vision seemed to focus. "Ah, my good brother," he sighed. "Everyone has been so good to me. Catholics, Orthodox, our own Confessing Church people have tried so hard. I would never have dreamed of such unity."

"Out of our caldron of pain, Christ has melded us together into one people," Christian agreed, mopping Ludwig's forehead.

"I tell you truly that I can now die in peace, knowing that I have seen the real body of Christ revealed as I have never known it before," he said, speaking haltingly. "Now I understand the promise of Jesus that we are to be like a storehouse that produces both the old and the new."

"What are you saying, Ludwig?"

"God has given me a new vision of the church, Christian! I now know that the Holy Spirit does remain as the true continuity between God's people of the past and God's church of the future." His face seemed radiant, his voice more intense.

"Our suffering is not without meaning, Christian. The old and the new are all intermingled here at Dachau." Ludwig

156

gripped his hand tightly. "What we have experienced has stripped away the barriers of the past and made all of us one in Christ."

"Perhaps that is exactly what Paul meant, when he said we are to complete in ourselves what is lacking in the suffering of Christ, to redeem His church."

"Yes, yes, yes." Ludwig gripped him harder. "God has graciously allowed us to be part of the redemptive work that can only come through the Cross. Something new will come out of these days that will purify not only us, but the whole church that comes after us."

"You did *not* shrink back, Ludwig! You *never* shrank back, my friend."

Ludwig dropped back against the rough board bed. His last words had come as a final sigh. His energy was spent; nothing more remained. The frail fingers loosened their hold and his momentary radiance vanished. Rest crept across his face.

As Christian watched Ludwig die peacefully, he saw all the faces of his deceased friends come together in that pale countenance. Long ago he had dealt with his bitterness and hate. Somewhere in the ensuing years, he had come to an acceptance of the inevitable. Yet Ludwig had taken him to still another plateau. Meaninglessness had turned to purpose. Out of the void had come eternal direction.

"Now you have helped me see the future of the church," Christian spoke to his friend's unhearing ears. "From all of these lifeless bodies will arise tomorrow's people of God as surely as our Lord walked out of His tomb! Though we have died surrounded by bitterness and evil, we are being resurrected in love and compassion. The new is coming!"

Very tenderly, Christian reached over and closed Ludwig's eyelids, and folded his arms across his chest. "Your courage will not go unrewarded, my friend. Out of your bravery, God will bring the new day."

CHAPTER TEN △

BABYLON
IS FALLEN—1945

One

THE FIERCENESS OF WINTER had passed, but the full warmth of spring had not yet come. However, for the second of April, the weather felt good.

Most of the men were still getting ready for roll call when a tall German policeman entered the Pastors' Barracks. As the men realized who he was, the room fell silent. SS guards were always expected, but a policeman seldom came unless there was unusual trouble.

Sensing their fear, the policeman announced loudly, "I have good news. Many of you are to be released today!"

"What? Who? Today? Is it me?" A hundred inquiries resounded through the room.

"Quiet! Quiet!" the policeman demanded. "I have a list of names and I will read them to you. Now, quiet!"

The press of the group brought Christian so close that he could read over the policeman's shoulder. As he scanned down the page, his eyes leaped ahead looking for only one thing. There

159

on the bottom of the second page was 26 661 and his name!

"We are being freed! We are being freed! We are being freed!" became the ecstatic litany. Men congratulated and hugged each other, weeping unashamedly.

In his joy, one pastor with an artificial leg hopped about the room, unaware that he had dropped his wooden limb on the floor. He began to shout, "The psalms promise, 'God, You have given to my feet an open ground!' "

"We have survived!" Christian told Gruber. "We have endured!" he yelled to Dittner, laughing and crying at the same time. "We're going to live, to leave! We have survived!"

Fearing the news might be too good to be true, the prisoners quickly gathered together everything they had and fell in behind the policeman. Only a few Bibles, eyeglasses, and some articles of clothing were left stacked around the barracks.

Each man wanted to be as close to the front of the line as possible. Some final door might yet shut before they all got out.

"Line up and stop pushing!" snapped the policeman. Instantly, the men fell into ranks and waited quietly for his instructions.

"All right, follow me!" For one last time, the group marched up the bunker. Here and there a final wave of good-bye signaled a friend that release had been obtained. Most of the prisoners watched the freedmen pass with little show of emotion. Many seemed dazed and unable to respond. Overhead, the black smoke of the crematoriums filled the sky. In between each barracks were corpses stacked in piles. Christian's eyes moved in a steady rhythm between the smoke and the bodies. While he couldn't keep from looking, he could no longer react to the routine side of Dachau.

Their line marched on to the assembly square, passing the SS pay office. Lieutenant Boye stood looking out the window, with Knoll behind him, peering over his shoulder. Boye made no gesture, only stared at a point on the horizon. Christian nodded his head and waved, but the SS officer appeared not to notice.

"Here I am being released," Christian remarked, turning to Dittner, "and yet I think that maybe Boye has become the prisoner now." Once more, he tried to get the lieutenant's attention. Knoll held his hands up in the air and made a victory gesture. Christian waved back, as one does in bestowing a blessing.

"I wonder what will become of Knoll?"

"What will become of any of them?" Dittner shot back.

The group abruptly halted as the policeman began exchanging papers with the SS officer.

"Why *are* we being released," Christian asked the men around him, "when these others are being left?" His euphoria of freedom was momentarily jolted by the realities of life with the SS.

"Perhaps someone has paid to get us out," a man on his left answered.

"Perhaps the Allies are almost here," another man ventured.

"If that were so," Dittner retorted cynically, "they would either be releasing everyone or killing us all!"

The wrought-iron gate swung open and the column of men tramped through. On the other side were the trucks they had hoped to see. As if being swept through a dream, Christian kept pushing forward as fast as possible. His hand was deep in his pocket tightly clutching the little bit of money he had been able to save and hide over many months.

"You will be taken to the train station in Munich," the policeman announced again and again as the men were loaded into the convoy trucks. "Quickly. We have no time to waste."

"For the first time in five years," Reger laughed nervously, "I am glad to be in a hurry!"

When the camp trucks dumped the men in front of the bustling Munich station an hour and a half later, no one even seemed to notice their arrival. Once again, Christian moved quickly in a final grab for freedom. This time there were no guards, no fences, no restraints. His mouth went dry; his heart beat fiercely; his breath came in great gulps.

The smell of smoke was still in the air from the bombing raids of the night before and an atmosphere of gloom hovered low. People appeared interested only in getting to safety. As the rest of the prisoners poured into the station house, the two old friends were left facing each other.

"You are no longer 26 661," Dittner spoke first. "You have again become Christian Reger."

"And you are free, my friend."

"I sense that we will never see each other again."

"Perhaps, perhaps . . . " Christian said hesitantly.

"Well, Christian, what have you learned through all of this?"

For a moment he felt the cynicism that was always latent in Dittner's questions. Christian studied the thin, drawn face of his fellow pastor whose eyes were as hard and bitter as ever.

"What have *you* learned, my friend?" Christian answered.

"I have learned how to remember. My mind will hold every detail of Dachau until every last atrocity has been vindicated. I know you would wish that I might tell you I have learned to forgive. It's not that you are not right, but the only force that has sustained me has been my hate. Perhaps, in the end, it will consume me." He grasped Christian's hand with both of his. Where coldness was usually etched on his countenance, trouble and pain suddenly infiltrated. "When I leave this train station, vengeance will be burned in my heart. If it takes my last breath, I must not cease to fight until National Socialism and Nazism are eradicated from the face of the earth and justice has been done!"

Christian looked down the long tracks that led out of Munich and to his destiny beyond. The converging rails seemed to pull his whole being far away from this gateway into hell.

"Well," Dittner asked with a heavy sigh, "what did *you* learn?"

Christian was pensive, then looked at Wilhelm with compassion. "Justice and vengeance for what we have seen is beyond comprehension. It isn't possible. These matters must be left in God's hands. But I know this—the world will not be made better by any more killing."

Dittner gripped his hand more tightly. "I cannot help myself. I must go on with this fight. I will never forget what they have done to us and our friends. I do not know how to forgive such . . ." and his words trailed off.

"Wilhelm, your soul has been shriveled. These years have made you hard. Haven't we seen enough tragedy without that?" Christian covered his friend's hands with his own. "How can we ever spread the story of love by talking and thinking of killing people?"

"And what have these endless years done for you?" Dittner's voice had become quiet and low.

"I don't know," Christian said slowly. "Right now, I only feel broken. All I can do is continue to trust God and walk one step at a time."

Instinctively, he grasped his friend's lapel and pulled him closer. "But we must not hate! If we do, they will have won because they will have been able to make us like them. Unless we are faithful to the way of love, there is no hope left for any of us!"

"And what is our hope?" Dittner asked haltingly.

"Our hope is that our courage has been honest and true—that we did not shrink back."

"Are you still so sure that you know what honesty and truth are?"

"Perhaps that has always been the difference between us. You must believe that you know. But me—no, I'm not sure about these things. I don't absolutely know that I am right."

Dittner's eyes filled with tears. "I guess," he said, biting his lip, "that is what has always made you a man of true courage."

He hugged his friend as Jonathan might have hugged David. "Good-bye, Christian. I will never forget you. God bless you! God bless you!"

Dittner quickly turned and ran down the platform, disappearing into the crowd. Christian wanted to say something more, but no words would come.

He seemed strangely rooted to the ground. He had longed for this moment, yet felt immobilized by the choices before him. Finally, his mind began to form a plan of action: the only way to reach Stieglitz would mean going through Berlin. If any rail routes were open, they would be coming out of the capital. In the next moment he rushed into the ticket office. The few deutsche marks Mina had been able to send in her last letters had been carefully hidden. Most of the savings of many months was quickly and gladly spent.

Only after the train had pulled away from the city was he fully able to believe that he would not be taken back to the camp at the last minute. Settling back against the seat, the scenery blurred before his eyes. He was almost unable to grasp that just a few hours earlier he had been beginning another hellish day at Dachau.

Then another realization struck him. "I could have taken Helmut's Hebrew Bible out with us!" he moaned. "What a significance it would have had in reminding us of his courage and of what our resistance had meant!"

To his surprise, as he calmed down, he found himself giving in to irresistible drowsiness, then heavy sleep.

Suddenly, he was crashing into the seat in front of him! Not awake enough to know what was happening, the next moment he found himself thrown onto the aisle. The train came to a grinding halt, sending people and luggage in every direction.

The windows began to explode, glass splattered, and gaping holes in the metal coach ripped open A man in front of

Christian seemed to be picked up by an invisible force and flung over the top of the seats.

"Down!" shouted someone upfront. "Everybody stay down!"

Then, for the first time he heard the airplanes. They were circling back for another attack.

Machine-gun fire began hitting other cars just before the rear of the train rocked with a gigantic explosion. As quickly as they had come, the planes were gone again.

"Now run!" a man in an army uniform screamed. "Run before they attack again. American airplanes are everywhere!"

People scrambled for the windows and the doors. In the frantic escape Christian realized just how slow and weak he had become. Falling from the coach stairs to the ground, he picked himself up and began running as best he could for a clearing rimmed by large trees. Halfway up the embankment he saw the airplanes coming back for a third strike.

It was as if a swarm of hornets were descending on a defenseless party of picnickers. Dirt began to fly and the field erupted. Everything disappeared into blackness and pain.

Two

Christian tried to focus his eyes, but his surroundings kept slipping away into unending dizziness.

"Please try to wake up!" pounded at his ears.

At last he began to recognize the shape of a man in a white coat standing over him.

"Try to wake up!" the man insisted.

Above him was a white sky. No, it was a white ceiling and around him were white walls. They were all too white and sterile to be the infirmary. To his astonishment, he began to recognize that some of the nurses were women.

"Where am I?" he asked, almost fearing the answer.

"You are in the hospital."

"I am your doctor," the man in white answered. "You keep asking for a capo. What is a capo?"

"The train? Yes, I was on a train."

"Where have you been?" the doctor wondered in consternation. "You look terrible. I've not seen many people in such emaciated condition!"

Christian didn't answer. He couldn't. He still couldn't comprehend what was happening.

"Your leg is going to be all right," the doctor continued.

"My leg?" For the first time Christian sensed the extreme soreness on the whole right side of his body.

"Yes," the doctor explained. "A piece of shrapnel went through your right leg. However, we have removed any pieces of metal and put your leg in a cast. In several weeks, it will be fine."

"Exactly where am I?" Christian asked.

"You are in the town of Bamberg," the doctor said as he made notations on his chart. "Like all of Germany, we have severe limitations on our rations. However, I am assigning you a special diet. It is important that you receive proper nourishment or your malnutrition will have worse effects than the bullet."

Christian lay back in bed and let his hands reassure him that he was really on a mattress with fresh sheets. He could almost feel the cleanliness around him. There was no shouting, no SS guards, no stench of crematorium smoke. He drifted into a deep, restful sleep.

Several weeks passed before he fully realized that this detour had probably saved his life. The rest and good food had restored him. Without any significant amount of money and in such poor condition he would not have lasted long out on the street. At the end of a month, he was not only walking again, but he felt stronger and healthier than he had in years.

During those weeks in the Bamberg hospital, the news came in avalanches of significance. The Russians had taken Berlin and Hitler had committed suicide. An unconditional surrender was declared by Germany and the Third Reich ended.

No one knew anything about prisoners at Dachau. Often he wondered what the SS had done to the men during the final days. Had they too been released? Or had something terrible happened? Uncertain of his own security, he was afraid to ask.

Day after day, from the hospital window, he watched waves of disposed, displaced, disillusioned people wandering through the streets. A world and a way of life had come to an end and no one knew the future. Germany was like an army with no general, no strategy, and no hope.

When he hobbled down the steps of the hospital and joined the stream of destinationless travelers, there was one thing of which he was sure. He had to find Mina. He had to get to Berlin.

Three

"No one will ever know how many of our leaders were killed," Bishop Dibeilius said, handing Christian a cup of coffee. "The SS had many of our pastors placed in the front lines. They were used as cannon fodder to slow the advance of the Russian army. At Stalingrad, many of these faithful men simply vanished in the wave of death and destruction that swept over the entire German infantry."

"I understand." Christian tried to balance the cup on his stiff leg. "And here in Berlin?"

"The fanatic fools fought to the very last ditch," the bishop answered, sitting down across from him. "Of course, the city

167

was turned into rubble and, again, many of our leaders perished."

"I would like to inquire about the fate of several friends. Would you know what happened to Dietrich Bonhoeffer?"

"I have difficult news to tell you. We have heard from Flossenburg Prison that our faithful brother was hanged shortly after you were released from Dachau."

Christian stirred his coffee without looking up or even acknowledging what he had heard.

"His release was only days away," the bishop continued. "Perhaps, in his death, his witness will be magnified far more than it would have been in his survival."

Christian stirred his coffee even more vigorously.

"Also, I must tell you other bad news that I have been asked to convey. Your friend Karl Leisner has died of tuberculosis."

Head still bent, Christian asked softly, "How did you find out?"

"The Dachau camp was liberated about the time you left Bamberg. Karl was taken to a hospital, but he died very quickly."

"I see."

"Christian, you must know that your faithfulness has not been in vain. Many remember what you did there."

"I did nothing!" Reger shouted. "I did nothing, I tell you!" His hands began to shake so violently that he could scarcely hold the cup. "I only survived. Would to God these good men would have lived rather than me!" His tears choked out his words. "I did nothing," he mumbled again, dropping his chin against his chest. He was frightened and bewildered by his own response. Yet the thought that he had lived when these others had died was unbearable. His very existence accused him of some nameless crime.

"If it is possible, Karl Leisner's family would like us to bring you for his burial."

"Where will it be?" Christian managed to ask.

"There is an old church in Xanten containing a grave of a Christian soldier who died during the Roman persecution in 303. Karl will be buried in that exact same grave."

"Oh, how very appropriate," Reger said, regaining his composure. "Once more, the old and the new are coming together. In his death, Karl will forever be a witness to our continuity with the true faith." His voice trailed off.

The bishop let the silence do its work. "Of course," he began again, "I know you want me to help you return home."

Christian looked up and set his coffee cup aside.

"Don't do it!" the bishop warned before he could speak. "The Russians are in complete control in Pomerania and no one knows what they will do."

"I'm sorry, but I cannot rest until I have found her."

"You have not heard from her in a long time," the bishop argued. "Perhaps she is no longer there. Refugees are everywhere."

"No," Christian answered firmly. "I know she would wait for me if she were. . . . "

"People disappear when they get too close to the Russians," the bishop went on, ignoring the implications of the uncompleted sentence. "After all you have survived, you must not let them snuff out your light."

"Bishop, do you think that after what I have lived through, I do not trust God for each hour of the day? Can I trust Him any less for my wife's well-being?"

"They told me you would not be swayed. I have already prepared the documents for you to use in slipping behind the Russian lines. But I still fear for you."

"Thank you, thank you." Christian extended his hand.

Going to his desk, the bishop finished signing a letter and several documents, then carefully folded the papers and put them in a large envelope

"Whatever happens or whatever you find," he said, handing the papers to Christian, "promise me you will come back before making any final decisions about the future."

Four

"You are the pastor who was in Dachau Concentration Camp?" the Polish railway conductor asked suspiciously.

"Yes," Christian answered nervously. "I am trying to get to my home in Stieglitz."

"Can you prove it?"

Christian gave him the bishop's letter and documents.

After reading the letter carefully, the conductor reached out and shook Reger's hand with deepest respect.

"I will be more than glad to help you," he smiled. "Follow me."

As the conductor began walking across the railway tracks, he pulled from his pocket a dirty, worn picture. "See," he said, pointing to the photo of a group of boys with a young man. "That is me. And that was our leader and pastor. His name was Dietrich Bonhoeffer."

Christian reached for the picture.

"In 1927," the conductor continued, "Pastor Bonhoeffer came to our poor parish in North Berlin. The times were bad, but he took care of us in every way possible. Oh, yes, there was great unemployment and misery, yet he taught me how to believe and survive in a cruel world."

"I can't tell you what sharing this means to me," Christian replied.

"Now, each day I must cross the East German frontier, and the terror is always there. So I keep this picture of the man who was my best friend with me, to remember what he taught."

170

"He and I were about the same work."

"Yes, I know. You must worry for nothing, for I will get you through. It is a small gesture on behalf of the memory of my friend." They entered the back door of the luggage car where the Polish conductor hid Christian in a corner behind a large pile of boxes.

"Do not move until I return for you. All Germans will be ordered off the train at Küstrin, but I will keep you hidden."

Later, after what seemed an interminable wait at the Küstrin station, the train started to move again, the click of the wheels against the rails getting louder and louder. Only a few hours more and he would be with Mina.

But would she be there? Were his friends' warnings valid? Perhaps all Germans would have been driven out of the village. Question after question raced through his mind—all except one. He could not even consider whether she was alive or not. When that thought would arise, he refused to let it linger.

Yet one thought would not leave him. What if *all* the Germans were gone? What if he got off the train into a village controlled by Russians? Might he disappear even as he entered his own hometown?

Finally, the uncertainty forced his decision. He would disembark at a stop about fifteen minutes before Stieglitz. If he walked into town, he would not be as easily identified.

Leaving the train unnoticed, he began the long trek home. He and Mina had come this very same route as a young couple on their way to their first church.

Five

Before him lay Stieglitz in late spring green. The steeple of his church still towered over the rest of the village.

Suddenly, crashing through the trees, a herd of cattle thundered only a hundred meters in front of him. Behind them came two Russians on horseback, driving the cattle across the tracks.

Christian froze, terrified that the Russians would turn on him, but they didn't even appear to notice as they vanished into the next field.

Reger started to run now. He knew he could see his house from the train station. Leaping onto the platform to get a clear view, his heart sank. There in the distance, all he could see were the charred remains. The stone fireplace and chimney were still standing, but the rest was rubble. Most of the surrounding houses were completely gone.

He stared in stunned silence.

"Can I help you?" asked a young girl, standing in the shadows of the station house. A small child was cradled in her arms.

"Oh, you startled me! I didn't see you."

"You are looking for someone?" She walked forward. "You are not a Russian?"

"No, no," he assured her. "I once lived here. But I don't remember you."

"I have come from another village to take care of the children that were left."

"Left?"

"Yes," she explained, as she rocked the baby. "In January, the Russians came very quickly and attacked one of the passenger trains, killing all the people."

"Why?" he asked in dismay.

"That is the way of the Russians. This is one of the children who survived when her parents were killed," she said, holding up the baby. "Now we do the best we can."

From the back of the station a man appeared, pedaling a bicycle. Christian had never seen the type of uniform that he was wearing.

"He is a Polish policeman," the girl answered in reply to

Reger's puzzled look. "I'm sure he can help you."

The policeman put down the bicycle and came toward them.

"I am looking for my wife," Christian said defensively. "Her name is Mina Reger."

"Of course, of course!" the policeman said, bowing as though a dignitary had just arrived from Berlin. "I am delighted you have returned. I will get her at once." He leaped on the bicycle and rode straight toward the village.

"Who are you?" the girl asked apprehensively.

"I was the pastor here once."

"Pastor Reger!" she said in amazement. "You are the one who has been a prisoner of the Gestapo!"

"You know of this?"

"Oh yes. Everyone in the village knows about you and your wife."

"My wife? You know of my wife?"

"Your wife is a wonderful woman," she said reverently. "Though others left when the Russians came, your wife stayed and kept many of us alive. Your wife is one of the bravest women I have ever known."

"Where can I find her, please?" Christian pleaded, his hands outstretched.

"When the houses were burned, she gathered the women into the mill and has been staying with them there. The Russians have violated so many of our women."

"Was she, ah, was she, I mean, is she all right?"

"The Russians never hurt her. Because they knew you were an enemy of the Nazis, they have shown her respect. In fact, she has been able to intercede for us many times."

"Thank God!" he said, suddenly embracing the girl. "Thank God she is all right." Hugging the child too he added, "Thank you, thank you so much for what you have told me!"

Reger jumped from the platform in full stride.

"Where are you going?" she called after him.

"To the mill!" he shouted back over his shoulder, running as hard as he could. "To the mill!"

He was almost to the edge of the houses when he saw Mina running down the lane toward him.

"Christian! Christian!" she shouted. "Here I am, here I am!"

"Mina, Mina," he yelled. "I'm back!"

"O Christian!" she sobbed. "My husband, my husband, my beloved husband. You really *are* alive!"

No words would come from his mouth. As the tears ran down his cheeks, he held her, kissed her, and clutched her as tightly as he dared.

As Christian looked mistily into her eyes, he realized how deeply the years of separation had etched their wear in her face. She was much thinner and her hair was grayer. Yet the toll of worry and care in no way obscured her beauty.

Christian had no idea how long they stood there. Time stopped, and in those moments, the weight of five years melted away. The agonies of cruelty and fear were lost in sheer joy.

They had each other again and nothing else mattered.

CHAPTER ELEVEN   △
A WORLD COME
TO ITS END—1945-46

One

AS THEY FINALLY DRIFTED off to sleep, the sun was rising over their little village. Each moment had been seized as if another might not follow. In their five long years of separation, a lifetime of experiences had transpired. Countless stories remained to be told. But in the end, having each other had crowded out all awareness of fatigue.

That afternoon they walked through the village, and at each burned or destroyed house, Mina told of the fate of the family. Amidst these streets that should be as familiar as his hand, Christian felt strangely displaced. The old world of his past had been swept away and in its place ruin and debris remained.

"Of course, the schoolteachers were the worst," Mina said, standing before one devastated dwelling. "They did not cease to teach racism to the children and to harass the parents about following the Nazi line. In the end, most of the people brought back their Confessing Church membership cards."

"The teachers always fought us during the church elections," Christian remembered.

"Many of the people were very irate about your arrest, but they soon turned away when the Gestapo applied pressure. They lost the courage of their convictions when it began to cost them personally."

"I know that must have been a terrible experience for you," he said, pulling her head to his shoulder.

"Often I would almost choke on my anger! To think my husband was in a concentration camp and they were afraid to carry a little piece of paper!"

They turned and walked to the church.

"My trumpeters?" he inquired. "What became of all those young men who played in our little band? I remember so well the excellent impression they always made on the townspeople when we performed."

"1933!" she said, walking up the steps. "Is it possible that you began that little group that long ago? Well," she continued sadly, "they are all gone. Every one of them marched off to war in their magnificent uniforms to fight the Russians. None ever came back. Most of their bodies were not even returned."

Stopping in front of the door, Christian looked down on the broad, stone stairway. "I remember how Wilhelm Kralemann attacked me on this very spot. I can still see his beet-red face as he told me that I was a traitor for teaching his son that he ought to follow the Bible's teaching rather than the state's."

"He was a very powerful figure in the church. You risked a great deal by your courage."

"Oh no!" Christian laughed. "Such stands cost little."

"More than you knew, my dear husband. After you were taken, we discovered that Kralemann was a secret agent for the Gestapo." Mina turned the key, unlocking the door. "The people came to hate him. As the Russians approached, he disappeared. I'm sure he will never be seen again."

"Ah!" Christian exclaimed of the war-spared stained glass windows. "Such a magnificent sight!"

"I'm afraid the building is very cold," Mina apologized. "We have not lit a fire in here for a long time."

"Then it's time to tell the people that a fire has been kindled again," Christian said, slipping into the front pew. "I must begin by reminding them that the light cannot be extinguished and that the darkness is still being overcome."

He rose and walked to the pulpit. Slowly he let his hands run across the ornately carved wooden decorations. It was all the same; it was all so different.

"I never ceased to be their pastor. I learned to pray for every face in this parish, whether they were faithful or not."

Christian looked up at the radiant windows and then down at his wife who seemed so small and frail sitting in the shadows. "I prayed for you every day. Each Christmas I tried to make my best prayer a gift for you."

"I love you," she said quietly.

Losing himself in their silent exchange, he murmured, "Even such words are not enough."

Each continued to silently look at the other, searching for some small assurance that they would still be together tomorrow and the day after that and the day after that.

"We will start again," he finally said.

"And I will play the organ."

"Spread the word that this Sunday at 9 o'clock there will be a fire in this church."

Two

Following the service, a small woman in a black coat and headscarf lingered at the door. It was Maria Schuster. Christian could sense that she wanted to say something to him that would be difficult and emotional. After the last person left, she moved down the aisle toward him.

"Please forgive me," she said, and quickly covered her eyes with an old handkerchief.

"Why, what in the world for?" he asked.

"My husband and I supported the SS, and we caused you problems that you do not even know about." She buried her face in her hands.

"The past is past," he consoled. "God has given us all a new day. None of us must look back."

She began crying more openly and reached for his arm. "My husband is gone; my house has been destroyed; and yet, when I remember the terrible problems we caused, I still can't forgive myself."

"We must let God's forgiveness be sufficient."

"You see," she sobbed, "we were good friends of Wilhelm Kralemann and we let him influence us. He was the one behind the first Brown Shirt attack on your house. Wilhelm caused you to be arrested."

"I always thought so," he answered, "but I have forgiven all that long ago. Do you know what has become of that family?"

"Ya," she said, dabbing at her eyes. "He was wounded in the war and lost his left arm. God's judgment was truly upon him."

Christian groaned as he remembered that Kralemann had been a violinist and pianist.

"They left Stieglitz as the Russians were coming. Probably they just hoped to hide somewhere else in Germany," she explained. "Most Nazis just want to vanish."

"I wish their family no ill will," he assured her.

"I want you to know I am trying to be a new person, and your wife has truly been my inspiration. I've done bad things, but I did not know people could do what the Russians have done to me " Her face momentarily twisted in pain "But as we huddled together in that old mill, your wife's words and deeds were my salvation. I know that she knew about the terrible things we had done to your family, and yet she was the very presence of God with me."

As Mina came back through the front door, Maria rushed over and hugged her very tightly. Then she hurried down the stairs. The pastor and his wife slowly locked the building and left for Sunday dinner at a parishioner's home. Both walked silently along the streets, each savoring every moment of the morning.

"Come in! Come in!" Mrs. Schmidt quickly ushered Christian and Mina into her living room. "How honored we are to have our pastor and his wife for this first Sunday dinner!"

"The service was wonderful!" praised Wolfgang, vigorously pumping Christian's hand. "I must tell you that I was so deeply touched by your sermon. I simply can't express my feelings."

"Now, Wolfgang, we must not get into any discussions now," his wife scolded. "The dinner will get cold. Come in and sit down."

With a festive air of celebration, the pastor and his wife were accorded the seats of honor. Wolfgang explained how the liebfraumilch had been carefully saved for such a special occasion. After the blessing, he toasted the return of their spiritual leader and then the rather meager feast began.

"Pastor," Mrs. Schmidt said as they ate, "before long you will have to conduct some very sad baptism services."

"Ya," her husband agreed. "Almost every girl in this village was raped when the Russians invaded. Next fall many babies will be born."

"Those who resisted were treated worse," Mina added. "We had a burial service for the few girls who did deny them."

"One of the worst terrors," Mr. Schmidt continued, "came from the Polish laborers who had been brought into the area as prisoners of war. When they were released, they took vengeance on many of the German farmers."

"Remember all of the difficulty you had with Max Warnke?" Mina asked. "Because he was a wealthy farmer, he felt he could turn the church against you."

"Well," Mr. Schmidt interrupted before Christian could speak, "his wealth and big farm didn't keep him from retribution. The Poles took his farm and moved him right out of his own house!"

"You should know of the brave thing your wife did," Mrs. Schmidt told him.

"Please," Mina said. "I would like to forget all of those stories."

"No!" Mrs. Schmidt insisted. "We will not forget your courage. When we were all hiding in the old mill, one of the Russian laborers broke in."

"Ya," her husband added. "He was looking for the village policeman because he wanted to kill him."

"The constable?" Christian remembered how the policeman had risked his own life to warn Reger he would be arrested by the Gestapo.

"Ya," replied Mrs. Schmidt. "He was already gone, but his wife was still in the mill. So the Russian said he would kill her instead."

"Your brave wife leaped up and tried to stop him. Nevertheless, the man shot and killed her anyway.

"God has used your wife in a special way," Wolfgang concluded.

"And what became of the constable?" Christian asked quietly.

"He died very cruelly in a Polish prison camp," Mr. Schmidt answered, lowering his eyes to his plate.

"The church has never been so full," Mrs. Schmidt finally broke the silence. "Extra chairs had to be placed in the back."

"Our people are starved for spiritual nourishment," Wolfgang went on. "Everyone is afraid that the Communists may even restrict our worship. We have not seen the end of our miseries."

"No," Christian agreed. "The future may be even worse."

"Communist domination is the new fact of life," Mina said. "Every day German families are being driven out of their homes. Regardless of the weather or time of day, a family may be put out on the street."

"Ya," Christian repeated, "the future may be even worse."

Three

A cold fall rain had begun to run down the window and the trees were swaying in the wind as Mina peered out. The vacant house where they had taken up residence was damp and dreary, but it was more than many of their fellow villagers could claim. "Christian, I think there is a plan behind these evictions."

"Ya, I have come to the conclusion that more is afoot here than Polish refugees needing shelter."

"I suspect that the Russians and Poles are systematically pushing all Germans out of the area. But many of our people have absolutely nowhere to go. I fear what will become of them."

"Because I opposed the Nazis, they have not persecuted us. Who could have expected that our enemies would be swept away and that in the end we would be in the privileged position?"

"See," Mina said, pointing across the street. "That poor woman has been pushed out of her house."

Looking through the sheer curtains, they saw a bent and aged widow walking dejectedly toward the train station. Across her shoulder she balanced a long stick with all of her possessions tied in a bundle on the other end.

"She is the last of her family," Mina observed. "Everyone else was killed in the war.

"Perhaps even we will have to leave before long," she ventured after a minute.

181

"Pastor! Pastor! Come quickly!" Hobbling up the stairs was one of the older women of the village who had also lost her entire family. "O Pastor," she cried, "you must come and help. It is horrible!"

"Calm down," Mina quieted. "Tell us exactly what happened."

"Oh, I can't!" she cried. "I cannot speak of this most horrible thing I have ever seen. Terrible! Terrible!" she choked.

As Mina and Christian both looked out the door, they could see a crowd gathering around a house at the far end of town. The woman only kept pointing in that direction. Not wasting another moment, husband and wife scurried off. The closer they came to the house, the louder the commotion. Germans and Poles were mingling together; everyone seemed agitated.

"What's happening here?" Christian asked one of the Germans. People stepped back to allow them through the crowd. Automatically, the entire group responded as if expecting the pastor to take control.

"Tragic!" a little man wailed. "Just tragic! To believe that people can be killed like this and nothing can be done!"

"Killed?"

"Ya," the man replied. "The old couple have both been murdered."

"Why?" Mina asked in disbelief.

"Polish robbers came to their house and wanted their sewing machine," he whispered. "When they resisted, the robbers killed them."

"O Lord," Christian moaned. "These old people killed over a sewing machine."

"They're in the bedroom," someone directed, as he and Mina entered the house.

"Stay in the living room," he told Mina firmly. "I will see."

Hesitantly, he looked around the corner into the bedroom. The old man's body was sprawled across the lifeless form of his wife. Near the window, where the sewing machine must have stood, was a blank space on the wall. A chair was overturned and two bullet holes shattered the plaster.

Outside, many of the new Polish tenants were staring through the windows. They were grinning and pointing, leering at the bodies. It was almost as though they had discovered a village carnival.

Christian looked around the room at the pictures of the old couple's children who were now somewhere far away. Perhaps they would never know about their parents' senseless murders.

Anger gripped him. Forcefully, he flung the curtains together and covered the bodies with the bedspread.

Giving one last long look around the room, he thought, *We cannot stay here much longer. These Poles and Russians don't value life any more highly than the Gestapo did.*

When he stepped outside, the crowd once more grew silent. The German faces seemed to beg for some word of direction; the Polish eyes were cold and suspicious.

"We will hold their funeral at the church tomorrow!" Reger said sternly. "They will be buried in the church cemetery. Let us make the necessary preparations." Taking Mina's hand, he abruptly walked through a cluster of Poles who quickly parted before him.

The day after the funeral, Christian returned to the graves. As he bent down to adjust some of the decorations, a rock sailed past his head. Another bounced off the gravestone in front of him.

"What is this?" he shouted indignantly, only to have another rock hit his coat.

Fifty feet away stood at least a dozen Polish peasants, rocks in hand.

Suddenly he charged at them, yelling at the top of his lungs, "How dare you throw rocks in this sacred place!"

One last rock whirred by as the group retreated over the fence.

Just beyond the church wall, they stopped to regroup and began hurling jeers instead. Christian stopped at the gate and realized just how many of them there were.

"Don't ever come here again without the proper respect!" he bellowed defiantly, at the same time feeling himself retreating in the face of what might happen.

The mob's jeers faded as they walked away. He knew well that only his opposition to the Nazis had kept him from worse. As he sat in his office considering the whole dilemma, Ursula Hinz bolted into the room.

"Pastor! Pastor!" she begged. "The Polish police have imprisoned my mother at Schönlanke. They may kill her!"

"Ya," Christian said sadly. "I have heard that Katie has been taken, but I am not sure there is anything I can do."

"Oh yes," Ursula urged, pulling at his coat. "You can let her know that I am alive and safe. My mother has no idea what has become of me."

"Of course," he answered. "Do you know why your mother was arrested?"

"For no reason except that my father was well known and in the German army. When they arrested her, they were very brutal," she explained, and began to cry again.

"My mother knows nothing of politics—everyone knows that. All the accusations against her are untrue!"

"Of course, of course. Go and tell Mina that I am going to Schönlanke and will be home late. I will do what I can."

When Christian arrived, he discovered that Frau Hinz was already in the courtroom, waiting to be tried. Cautiously, he got as close as he could to where she was seated.

As if speaking from the pulpit, he began, "And her daughter Ursula has come home. Even now she is in quite good health."

People turned to see who was talking so loudly.

"Ya," he continued, "her daughter Ursula is home and is fine."

Katie Hinz found his eyes and smiled pleadingly. The broken-
ness etched on her face gave way to gratitude.

"Ya," he started again, then sensing that people were staring at
him as if he were a spy or crazy, his voice dropped. "Ya, she is
fine." Several men eyed him as if action should be taken. After a
few minutes, Christian edged out of the room.

Two days later, he discovered that Frau Hinz had died from
harsh treatment.

Four

"Christian!" Mina called into the church office. "Come quickly!
Look who is here!"

As Christian stepped out of his study, a pale-complected man
extended his hand. "Paul Hartwig!" he exclaimed. "You are alive
and well!" Reger embraced his old friend.

"Christian, how wonderful that you have survived these terrible times."

"I want you to know," said Mina, "that Paul was one of the
very few who did not turn in his red card. He stayed with us
through it all."

"I am so grateful to you, Paul. Mina has told me that
eventually almost everyone lost their convictions. Where have
you been?"

"God is truly faithful to those who keep faith with Him.
Whatever small amount of courage I had, He has rewarded me
in far greater abundance than I deserve." He paused to catch his
breath, then added, "Only two of us escaped out of nearly
30,000 people."

"What do you mean?" questioned Mina. "You were not draft-
ed into the army."

"I have just come from Schneidemühl," Paul explained.

"Nearly all of the German people have been driven out of their homes and are being forced to walk to Russia."

"Thirty thousand people!" Christian exclaimed.

"Men, women, and children. God only knows what will become of them."

"Why?" Mina asked incredulously.

"Only because they are Germans," Paul said.

"How did this happen?" Mina continued to probe.

"Two days ago Russian soldiers began sweeping through the area, herding all the people together. Their loudspeakers told us we were all being sent to Russia and warned that resistance would be met with death. I knew I did not have the strength to survive such a journey."

"But, Paul," Mina asked, pouring him a cup of coffee, "how did you escape?"

"While everyone was being rounded up in the square, I walked behind the city hall. Kneeling down, I prayed, 'O Lord, You know my weakness. I know You worked miracles in the past and that You can work wondrous things today. Please help me in my hopeless situation!

"Then, somewhere in the distance, I heard my name. I realized I was being called by a loudspeaker. When I reached the Russian officer in charge, he told me that I and a Catholic schoolteacher would be released from the march. He sent us out of the town immediately."

"A schoolteacher?" Christian queried.

"Ya," Paul explained. "He was the only man who opposed the Nazis in the whole school system. Of the 30,000 people, only he and I were released."

"Your integrity saved you," Christian declared. "They recognized your resistance to the Nazis."

"Perhaps," Paul smiled, "but as I came here today, I kept remembering the last words of my mother. I believe her advice is the real reason I have survived."

Paul balanced the cup and saucer on his knee as he looked out the window toward the station. "Forty years ago, I brought my sick mother to that railway station, and she never came home from the hospital. But when I put her on the train, her last words to me were from Psalm 119. 'Don't forget!' she shouted from the window, 'How shall a young man steer an honest course? By holding to Thy Word!' Ever since, I have tried to live by His Word and that is why I have survived."

"You have kept the faith, Paul," Christian assured him. "You did not shrink back."

"Now I have come to warn you," Paul said, putting down his cup and standing to leave. "You must not stay here. As long as they remember that you opposed Hitler, you are safe. However, the Communists are worse than the Nazis. You must leave."

"Thank you, Paul," Christian answered. "We will consider your advice carefully."

"God bless you." As Paul started down the steps, he paused to turn and bid a final farewell. Each sensed he would not see the other again.

Five

The Schmidts were tying up the last of their bundles. Their walls had been stripped of all the family pictures and each momento was carefully packed with their few dishes.

"We believe that we can still be on the evening train," Mr. Schmidt told Mina. "That will allow us to arrive in West Germany tomorrow afternoon."

"Your children will be there to meet you?" Christian asked.

"Ya," Mrs. Schmidt sighed. "We are so much more fortunate than most. Our family will help us get settled again."

"Stieglitz will not be the same without the Schmidt family."

"Well," Mr. Schmidt replied with a sorry smile, "Stieglitz will never be the same anyway. Everything we had here is changed. We are not leaving any too soon."

"How did it all happen?" Mrs. Schmidt wondered. "Such a few years ago everything was happy and good."

"You forget the depression," Wolfgang reminded his wife. "Times were hard and food was scarce!"

"Then Hitler promised us that he would solve every problem," Mina added. "People believed he could do anything."

"We became a nation of little Hitlers," Mrs. Schmidt commented bitterly. "Everyone believed he had a right to land, to power, to anything he wanted."

"It was that radio!" Mr. Schmidt accused. "Hitler was constantly in our living room. None of us ever had our own radios before National Socialism came to power. Because we could hear his voice, we believed everything he said."

"No," Christian said sadly. "People believed because they wanted to believe. Fear and selfishness produced a ready-made audience for fanaticism."

"Oh, you are so right!" said Mrs. Schmidt, picking up a thick red book from the table. "See this book? I have just been reading Dostoyevski again. Here," she said, holding the page to the light. "Listen to how much this sounds like Hitler. 'The Grand Inquisitor succumbs to the dread spirit of death and destruction, and, therefore, accepts lying and deception, and leads men consciously to death and destruction, and always deceives them, so that they do not know where they are being led, and all the time these poor, blind creatures believe themselves to be happy!' Is that not a perfect description of what *we* have lived through?"

Christian felt the blood rushing to his face. He tried to measure his words so that his emotion would not show. Yet she had pulled from him the one question that remained unanswered. "Did you have any idea that the Nazis were torturing us at Dachau and that people were being gassed? Did you know they were killing Jews?" The room became uncomfortably silent.

"Of course not!" reacted Mrs. Schmidt. Her voice sounded both embarrassed and offended. "We knew nothing of these terrible atrocities!"

Christian said no more, but turned slowly toward Mr. Schmidt. For reasons he couldn't quite understand, he was suddenly angry with these people who had helped him so much during the past weeks.

Wolfgang avoided Reger's eyes and began to adjust the pile of boxes. After a moment he answered, "I can honestly say I did not know of these things, Christian. But I must confess that I also did not *want* to know of any of those things.

"I'm sorry," he continued. "Perhaps we could have known if we had wanted to. Maybe this will be our eternal curse. We did very little to stop the spirit of death and destruction when it came."

Finally, Mrs. Schmidt added, "Is not our having to leave suffering enough?"

Mina gave Christian a look that clearly said, "No more." Realizing that they might not see these people again, she moved the conversation in other directions. Quickly, their possessions were loaded in a wagon and they were gone.

"Schmidt was right," Christian told Mina as they walked back to the house where they were staying. "Stieglitz will never be the same again. I think it is time to go. I am not afraid of the problems, but I believe our work here is finished."

"You have changed," Mina mused as she grasped his hand. "The time at Dachau has made you different."

"How?" he asked in a troubled tone.

"Oh," she laughed, "it is all good. You were always a strong person, but often too naive and innocent. You thought everybody was good. Life was very simple for you."

"That was bad?" he asked.

"No," she replied. "But now you are different. Your sermons are so strong they make me weep. The innocence and naiveté have been replaced by an honesty and candor that can cut to the bone. You leave people confronted in a way that is startling and confounding."

"I am too blunt?"

"No. What you say is good. I just find that you have seen the truth about people and power in a way few ever do. Through it all, your faith has become complete."

"Oh no," he objected. "Far from complete. Perhaps confident is a better word. God gave me an experience of His light long ago. In seminary He showed me how He could dispel the darkness of my doubts. I suppose that now I know He can dissolve the darkness of my fears as well."

They walked in twilight past the burned ruins of their old parsonage. "I think it is time for us to go home and begin to pack," he concluded as they reached the house. Resolutely, he closed the door behind them.

CHAPTER TWELVE △
THE PESTILENCE RETURNS—1946

"WELL, I don't want to rush you, but you have been staring at that door for about five minutes."

The annoyance in the bishop's voice jolted Christian's mind back to the moment at hand.

"I asked you if you would agree to serve a church in the Communist-held sector of Berlin," Bishop Dibeilius repeated.

"I'm sorry," Christian apologized, slowly pulling his gaze from the huge door in front of him, "but there are so many things in your office that bring back memories."

"Oh?" The older man raised his eyebrows.

"Yes. Perhaps simple things like matchboxes and doors help me most in thinking about what is involved in saying a simple yes."

Opening the red and green matchbox, the bishop lit his pipe.

Before he could speak again, Christian asked, "I know this sounds unusual, but might I have that matchbox?"

"The matchbox? Well, of course," he said, handing it to Christian. "Keep it if you wish."

"Why should I go?" Christian inquired, looking at the box in his hand. "Why should I enter such a battle again?"

"Because the Dragon is not dead!" The bishop blew a puff of smoke high in the air. "And the Beast has been resurrected again in East Berlin. Perhaps I could say better that Communism is now the 'lamb that speaks with the voice of the Dragon.' The battle goes on and is not finished.

"So why should you enter again? I will tell you simply, my friend. Because you are a man of courage. As a soldier of the Cross, you have no choice. You cannot turn aside from this decision and still be who you are!"

The bishop smiled slightly. He knew he had finally found the right argument. He had won and the matter was settled.

Christian pursed his lips and exhaled deeply. He began slowly nodding his head up and down, even before he uttered a final affirmation. "If this is the call of Christ," he said very slowly, "I must say yes." Resolutely, he placed the matchbox in his pocket. "We will accept the appointment. We will go."

"Wonderful!" the bishop exclaimed as he returned to his desk and reached for his pen. "I will sign the letter and complete the instructions in order that you may go at once. You need not delay; the church will be expecting you. Even now, you could prepare for the move to the parsonage."

"We have virtually nothing to take with us," Christian admitted. "The few items we have are in boxes here in Berlin."

"Good! Good!" the bishop murmured without awareness of what he was affirming. "Then you could leave for the Eastern Sector this afternoon."

"I suppose so."

"Well then, let us go and tell your wife."

"Perhaps it would be better if I talked to her alone."

"Of course, of course," the Bishop conceded, shaking Reger's hand heartily. "We will be praying for you. Go in God's strength!"

Christian shut the door quietly behind him. Mina looked up

expectantly. The large waiting room with its high ceiling seemed to encase them in a solitude and privacy that felt like a momentary shelter in the midst of a continuing storm.

"Doors," he said to his wife. "Isn't it strange how the opening and closing of doors can change everything. The simple act of turning a handle can make all the difference."

"Then you said yes," Mina said, standing to greet him.

He looked down at the worn carpet and tried to avoid her eyes as he adjusted his glasses and fixed his tie.

"Are we going back into the danger?" Her voice betrayed no emotion.

"I do not want you to feel that your thoughts and feelings have no bearing on this decision. Certainly, I would not accept this appointment unless you were in agreement."

"What did you tell the bishop?"

"I am still not sure that such a treacherous environment would be right for you. After all you have suffered, I could not bear you having to once again live through a reign of terror."

"Of course," she said. "I need no reassurances. Did you say we would go?"

"Yes." He reluctantly raised his eyes to meet hers.

"Good!" she beamed. "You have made the right decision. Let us get our things together."

"But. . . . " He fumbled for more explanation. "But we will face certain persecution from the Russians. No one knows what is going to happen to Christians under a hostile, atheistic government."

"No one ever knows what is going to happen anywhere," she countered, reaching down for her handbag. "Since we can't choose such things, we must make our lives our own, wherever we are. Haven't we always done that?"

"Well, yes," he agreed, gesturing futilely. "But I felt that you might want to have an easier life, a more comfortable home."

"Comfort is a poor excuse for anything." She shook her finger in his face in mock admonition. "When were we ever called to comfort? Is not life more than what we eat and drink?"

"My, my," he smiled sheepishly. "Look who has become the preacher now! I simply needed to know that you wanted to go."

"Oh, we have suffered." Her face instantly became serious. "God knows we have suffered! Yet even in the worst days of our separation, we were still completely alive. No, I would not want to relive the past years, but I would not have missed them for anything. I know in whom I have believed and now I know that He is able. Never did we retreat from the conflict, and I know that our souls have been stretched and our characters refined by it."

"I am very proud that I have known you." He looked deeply into those marvelous, misty eyes that seemed so young again. "I thank God that He has made it possible for me to look just a little into your soul." Taking her face into his hands, he tilted it upward. "I was sustained by your love when everything else was dying. I drew life from you."

"Now, now." She seemed embarrassed. "You know that there is no place in the world that I would not go if I were going with you." She hugged him tightly and they let the silence express what was beyond words.

"Remember what happened when you held the first service after your return?" Mina began. "I can still see the packed sanctuary. Those desperate, frightened people clutched their Bibles as a drowning man hangs onto a rope. The cares and woes of the centuries were etched into their faces. I can still see all of those hollow children who had seen too much and whose innocence was forever banished. They strained forward to hear as if you were their only hope. We can never leave them behind. Surely, their tribe must wait for us in East Berlin."

He took his hat from the stand. "Well, our work is certainly cut out for us."

"Did the bishop say anything about the Confessing Church?"

"No, he carefully avoided the subject. I know the Confessing Church will always be a judgment on those who cooperated with the Nazis. Undoubtedly, many of those who followed National Socialism will be very uncomfortable with our witness."

"Maybe it would be best if our movement were absorbed back into the established church."

"Remember how the Danube begins in the Black Forest?" he asked, suddenly finding a perfect illustration. "Only a little stream bubbles up and then it disappears back into the ground. Yet it finally erupts into a great river that runs through many countries. Perhaps we Confessors will be like that."

"Arising in a great crisis," she smiled back, "only to disappear after the war; yet in other times and places when the cost is great, the work of the Confessors will go on and on."

"I think so. At Dachau I was part of a brotherhood of all Christians. There were no barriers between us. I hope others will remember that great lesson if ever an evil political power threatens the life of the church again."

"And like the Danube," she said, squeezing his hand, "we will be swept along together—one mighty army, beginning with the apostles, then enlisting the faithful of all generations, until we come as one people to that Final Day."

"Oh, I like that!" He squeezed her hand in return. "When I left Stieglitz, I felt like Lot leaving the burning city of Sodom. Perhaps the smell of burning will be upon us for many years. But like Lot, I know we have been saved and that angels have accompanied us. So, rather than remembering the smoke, let us recall that great flood of witnesses and remember the communion of the saints. These are the things we must tell people."

"Perhaps it would have been nice to return to a simple, quiet parish like Stieglitz was when we first went there," Mina said somewhat wistfully. "But then, life never really was routine. I suspect that God has some interesting plans ahead for us."

195

"Well, I guess you know that we go to enter a battle that we cannot win," Christian concluded.

"To gain a victory we cannot lose," she instantly responded.

Lovingly, he extended his arm and they walked across the waiting room to the door leading down to the street. Slowly he opened it, and the brisk, mid-April air rushed in to meet them.

She paused on the threshold. "Just going through a door can change everything."

"Indeed!" he smiled. "But then again, we have never been among those who shrank back!"

They walked down the broad, stone steps and onto the sidewalk. Ahead, a little boy was playing by the curb, and somewhere in the apartments above, a child was crying. The spring weather felt especially fresh and invigorating.

AFTERWORD △

... AND THEY DID NOT TURN BACK

ONLY IN LATER YEARS did Christian Reger and the world learn the full truth of what happened at Dachau Concentration Camp.

It is estimated that nearly 200,000 inmates from 37 countries went through the iron gates from 1933 to 1945. Three days before the camp was liberated, the Nazi index cards listed 30,442 men living in an area built to accommodate 5,000. While this statistic is grossly inaccurate, it reveals that even according to the records of the Third Reich, Dachau was torturously crowded beyond any capacity to provide minimal humane care.

Because so many Jews were shipped on to Buchenwald and other death camps, Dachau's population figures will always be obscure. After the Crystal Night in 1938, more than 10,000 Jews were sent to Dachau. While many of them were later able to leave the country, the fate of the rest will always be a mystery. Eighty children ranging in age from eight to fifteen arrived at the camp, yet all disappeared without reasonable explanation.

The inmate count of clergymen sent to Dachau is also unclear. At least 2,720 pastors from nineteen nations were incarcerated.

Ninety-five percent of those were Roman Catholic priests; 5 percent were Protestant. One third of all the priests of Poland died in the barbed-wire city.

The captured Nazi records verify that 360 to 400 inmates were used for the diabolical medical experiments of the camp doctors. Documentation proves that at least 3,166 men were gassed at Hartheim Castle in the Austrian city of Linz. At least 30,500 men died in the camp itself the final four months before freedom came.

On Sunday, April 29, 1945, while Christian was recovering in the Bamberg hospital, Dachau was liberated by American soldiers. National flags of many nations, made in secret, were unfurled and the camp was jubilant. For the first time, religious services were held openly and men rejoiced that the long night of terror was finally ended.

Emmerich Ost, the Dachau camp commandant, was killed in a Polish labor camp. A special trial was held in Dachau, charging Dr. Schilling with numerous medical crimes. He too was executed. As did many Nazis, Lieutenant Herman Boye disappeared "underground." Ironically, he later surfaced as a policeman.

The Confessors returned to the mainstream of German church life and the Confessing Church movement came to an end. Because they chose to forgive those who had unrightfully persecuted them and to forget the indiscretions of those who had compromised with the Nazis, a reunion was achieved in the German church.

Christian and Mina accepted the challenge of Bishop Dibeilius and went into the Russian sector of East Berlin where no one else wanted to serve. They lived through the turmoil and treachery of the Communist takeover, and domination of the city and its government.

Ten years after the liberation, the prisoners of Dachau returned for a commemorative service and decided to turn the camp into a permanent memorial. Catholic, Protestant, and Jewish centers of worship were planned. On April 30, 1967, the Protestant Church of the Reconciliation was dedicated as a symbol of the healing of hostilities.

Mina continued steadfast in her devotion to her husband and their call until her death on March 25, 1970. Using a quotation from the early church, Christian had carved on her small monument:

> TO YOUR BELIEVERS, O LORD,
> LIFE IS BEING CHANGED,
> NOT TAKEN AWAY.

The summer after her death, Christian returned to Dachau to become the pastor of The Church of the Reconciliation. For the next nine years, he told thousands of visitors about his experiences as a prisoner. In three different languages, he recounted the story of the matchbox, the Pastors' Barracks, and of the Light that darkness could not extinguish.

Through the years, visitors were inspired and moved by his witness. Countless letters of appreciation were received, including one from President and Mrs. Gerald Ford. Christian received a citation from the U.S. Army and was awarded the Order of Merit from the German government.

Failing health brought his complete retirement in 1979. Even in his final years, he remained always among those who kept the faith and did not shrink back.

In April 1985, a month after his 80th birthday, his heart problems worsened. For the next 22 weeks, Christian's deteriorating condition casued continual hospitalization. During much of this time his memory faded. But on Friday, October 11, Christian suddenly became alert and learned with deep satisfaction that this book would be published in the spring. The next day he quietly died in his sleep.

His obituary contained this poem:

> The beginning, the end,
> O Lord, are Thine.
> The span between,
> The life is mine.
> When in the night
> I lose my way,
> I seek Thy Light,
> Thy House, Thy Day.

SOLA GLORIA DEI

Christian Reger's Germany

International boundaries as of January 1, 1938

Miles 0   50   100   150

Kms 0   50   100   150   200

ENGLAND

DENMARK

North Sea

Hamburg

Amsterdam

NETHERLANDS

Münster

Xanten

Duisburg

Elberfeld

Sachsenhausen

Brussels

BELGIUM

GE...

Rhine River

Frankfurt

Compiègne

Mannheim

LUXEMBOURG

Hockenheim

Paris

FRANCE

Rhine River

Zurich

SWITZERLAND

LIECHTENSTEIN

Clermont Ferrand